ALPINES

Discover gardening in miniature with these
delightful alpines and rock garden plants

Geranium dalmaticum

Penstemon newberryi

A GARDENER'S GUIDE TO
ALPINES

Discover gardening in miniature with these
delightful alpines and rock garden plants

MICHAEL UPWARD

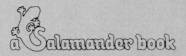

a Salamander book

Published by Salamander Books Limited
LONDON

A Salamander Book

Published by Salamander Books Ltd.,
52 Bedford Row,
London WC1R 4LR.

© 1988 Salamander Books Ltd.

ISBN 0 86101 380 8

Distributed by
Hodder and Stoughton Services,
PO Box 6, Mill Road, Dunton Green,
Sevenoaks, Kent TN13 2XX.

All correspondence concerning the
content of this volume should be
addressed to Salamander Books Ltd.

Contents

Text and colour photographs are cross-
referenced throughout as follows: 64 ▶

The plants are arranged in alphabetical
order of Latin name. Page numbers in
bold refer to text entries; those in *italics*
refer to photographs.

Credits

Author: Michael Upward has been Secretary of the Alpine Garden Society since 1961. He has travelled extensively to the mountain regions of the world in search of alpines – North-west America, Norway, the Swiss Alps, the Pyrenees, Italy, Sardinia and the Himalaya, to which he is shortly returning on an expedition searching for new plants to introduce to cultivation. He has also visited South Africa on several occasions to study the rich flora that abounds there. Michael is an occasional contributor to the gardening press on alpines. He is a keen gardener and writes from personal practical experience.

Editor: Geoff Rogers
Designer: Roger Hyde
Photographs: Those on pages 6 and 9 have been supplied by the author. All the other photographs have been taken by Eric Crichton exclusively for this book.
© Salamander Books Ltd.
Line Drawings: Maureen Holt.
© Salamander Books Ltd.
Colour and monochrome reproductions:
Bantam Litho Ltd., England.
Filmset: SX Composing Ltd., England.

Printed in Belgium by
Henri Proost & Cie, Turnhout.

Introduction

To choose a mere 156 alpines, out of a total of several thousand that could be grown, might appear at first to be a daunting task. It is certainly invidious to have to exclude some of the most attractive genera, but as the main criterion was the availability of the subjects in commerce, the exclusion of some of the rarer and more challenging plants was rendered somewhat easier, and reduced the list to more manageable proportions. Also excluded are any alpines that are tender, although there may be one or two borderline plants that in harsher climes could tend to curl up their toes at extreme temperatures.

However, the plants given here are, in general, basically hardy. Among the plants described there are several genera of which only a representative selection can be included. The campanulas, saxifrages and gentians come to mind, along with *Dianthus, Helianthemum, Lewisia, Penstemon, Phlox, Primula, Rhododendron, Sedum, Sempervivum* and *Thymus*; these would all repay wider study for the variation that is to be found within their ranks, in colour, texture and varying forms.

Dwarf shrubs have been scantily dealt with in the text. There are many that help to provide a background for the rock garden, such as *Berberis* × *stenophylla* 'Corallina Compacta', which is a perfect essay in miniaturization of the larger forms. The dwarf willows bring interest in late winter with their catkins, and *Salix* × *boydii* provides a variation with its delightful grey woolly leaves.

To dismiss a potential misunderstanding, the terms 'alpine' and 'rock plant' are synonymous. Consideration should be given at this point to the actual rock garden itself – the term 'rock garden' being infinitely preferable to 'rockery'.

The rock garden

The basic material, rock, is very expensive these days, and economical use must be made of the material available. It is not necessary to have a steep slope on which the rock garden can be built. It is possible to create one on a perfectly flat site, by excavating paths and piling up the excavated soil to make the rock garden. My own practice is to create a gentle slope and then arrange the rock on

Left: *A typical example of how plants colonise inhospitable sites in the wild. Here,* Geum reptans, *related to* G. montanum *in the text, is putting down roots in a seemingly soilless environment, but which in fact contains substantial nutrient in the crumbling detritus.*

Right: *An idea of an average rock garden situation with dwarf shrubs giving background interest and with good use being made of* Aubrieta, *a common, even despised, plant that is invaluable for spring colour. Remember to cut it back after flowering to maintain its neat clump.*

Above: *This drawing shows a cross-section of a rock garden. Drainage material and soil layers have been built up into a gentle slope and the rocks positioned as outcrops.*

Right: *The final stages of setting up an exhibition rock garden show the outcrop principle in use. The gentle slope has been topdressed with chippings between the rocks.*

the outcrop principle. To go back to basics for a moment: all rock starts off as a solid lump; nature then fractures it horizontally and vertically. In practice this means that one does not interlock rock as in a brick wall; rather, the lines should follow each other through.

The outcrop principle creates individual beds, which can then have different soil mixtures to accommodate the varying needs of certain plants.

No rock garden should be completed in a hurry, for trouble is bound to follow. It is essential to remove all perennial weeds from the site, resorting to chemical means if they are persistent; this advice cannot be emphasized too much, even if it does sound boring. Neither should there be any hurry to plant, as the ground needs to settle. Ideally the rock garden should be constructed in autumn, and left to settle over winter, planting in spring.

What sort of rock should be chosen? For practical, economic and aesthetic reasons it should be the rock that is quarried nearest to the site of your garden. If you are in a sandstone area do not choose limestone or vice versa, as it will look wrong. There is a light-weight substance called tufa, formed in some limestone areas, which is porous and much beloved by some plants, because they can get their fine roots into it.

Alpines do not have to be grown on a rock garden. An alternative is the raised bed, built of rock to whatever height is required. It is a most practical idea for elderly or wheelchair gardeners, as the plants are brought up to their level. Trailing plants can cascade over the sides, and those requiring good drainage can be planted on top. Such beds can also be constructed with old railway sleepers or breeze blocks, though the latter do not have quite the natural look about them.

The peat bed

The peat bed is constantly referred to and this is very much a man-made concept. The ideal situation is near water, to give a buoyant atmosphere. Here the rule about building a brick wall can apply, as interlocking gives strength to the peat blocks if they have to be raised at all. Some experts suggest that it is possible to create a

peat garden for acid-loving plants above an alkaline soil. My view is that you should not be trying to defeat nature all the time: if you live in an alkaline or chalky area, then accept the fact and grow what does well in your area, rather than have miserable plants struggling to live in adverse conditions.

The peat garden is for acid-loving plants and those that require cool moist conditions. Some shade, but not a total overcast, is also required, where plants can be protected from intense sun, particularly at midday in high summer. The dappled sunshine that filters through a deciduous tree is ideal. The peat garden can be separate or part of the general rock garden if the situation lends itself. Dwarf rhododendrons are very useful subjects, as there is such a vast selection of colour and form to choose from.

The terms 'alkaline' and 'acid' are used frequently. These are the extremes of the pH scale, on which 7 is considered to be neutral: anything below 7 is acidic, and above is alkaline. In practice it is rare to find a pH greater than 8.5 or lower than 4.5, although some moorland soils can go down to 3.5 or lower. No ericaceous plant will tolerate any alkalinity much above a pH of 6.5, but plants that tolerate a high pH will sometimes grow in acid conditions.

Troughs and sinks
Reference is occasionally made in the text to a plant's suitability for planting in a trough or sink. The ideal is the natural stone sink originally used in old cottages. In days gone by these could be obtained cheaply, but nowadays they have become almost collectors' items. These sinks accommodate the real miniatures and are a delight in a particularly small area or on a terrace or patio. It is not possible for everyone to obtain a natural stone trough, so a substance called 'hypertufa' was invented some fifty years ago. This is a mixture of sand: peat: cement in the ratio of 1:2:1 to give a tufa-like finish or 2½:1½:1 to give a sandstone finish. A trough can be made entirely of this substance by placing a layer of the mixture in the base of a cardboard box, placing another, but smaller, box on top of this layer; this should leave a gap all round, which is then filled with

more of the mixture and left. The 'give' of the cardboard boxes will provide some irregularity to the trough's appearance.

Alternatively, a glazed sink can be coated with the hypertufa, using an industrial adhesive. This can be a tricky operation, but a thin layer (5-10mm/0.2-0.4in) is spread on after coating the glazed sink with adhesive. It can be 'chipped' when almost dry to give a natural look.

Propagating frames

In the text, propagating frames are mentioned; these can be sited outside, either free-standing or against the walls of a house, shed or greenhouse. A sand frame is made up from pure sharp sand, kept moist, into which any cutting is inserted. Some plants prefer a cooler, damper medium, in which case the peat frame is recommended, with just a smattering of sand to keep it 'open'. Whatever the mixture, there is always a glass frame over it, to conserve the heat and to control the water supply. Ideally, the cuttings should be no more than 15cm (6in) away from the glass; tall cuttings are inserted at the back, as most frames are sloping. Sometimes propagating frames are placed in a greenhouse, and this offers double protection to less hardy subjects, but care should be taken that these cuttings are not drawn up by the combination of glass and heat.

'Pinching out' is a term used after propagation takes place. This simply involves the removal of the central growing point, to encourage the plant to sprout lateral shoots and in general to keep it looking neat.

Growing alpines from seed

Seed sowing is a straightforward operation, with less mystique than some tend to attach to it. The main thing is to choose the right type of container, ie clay or plastic and the correct size. Remember that plastic pots can easily be overwatered. Fill the pot to the brim with compost, tapping the pot to settle the compost; then, with another pot, press the mixture firmly so that there is a gap of about 6-7mm (0.24-0.28in) from the rim. Sow the seeds thinly; this is most important, as crowded seedlings are prone to damping off. Then cover with either sharp sand or chippings, according to the fineness of the seeds sown. Stand the pot in a bowl of water, with the level of water lower than the rim of the pot, until the surface of the soil glistens with moisture; you will then know that it has percolated through.

Seed and potting composts need a short explanation. There are two basic forms of these composts: the well-tried and well-known John Innes formula, and the peat-based Arthur Bowyers, the latter being more suitable for ericaceous and peat-loving plants. In commerce John Innes composts are extemely variable, but the Cal-Val brand can be recommended as excellent for alpines. Limestone and granite chippings can be added to the compost to cater for any plant's particular requirement: most saxifrages, for instance, thrive on good drainage and enjoy limestone chippings.

Always label seed pots with a reliable pen or indelible pencil, as some alpine seeds may not germinate for a year or two. If they have not germinated in the first season, leave the pot out to be frosted the following winter, to see if that will assist germination.

In general it is sensible to label plants on the rock garden, but a forest of white labels is not an attractive sight, so try to choose a less obtrusive type. Regrettably, metal labels are no longer manufactured, but if old stocks can be found they are ideal.

The alpine house

The alpine house is every enthusiast's eventual dream. It is devised to house plants that are not so much tender, as more in need of protection from adverse overhead weather, such as winter rain. No heating is necessary, and in fact considerable extra ventilation must be supplied to prevent a stagnant atmosphere from encouraging disease. It is only in the severest weather that the alpine house is shut up completely. Here can be grown some of the most challenging and difficult plants from the world's mountains. It is also a good place to be if the weather is too bad to garden outside or some unpleasant domestic chore needs to be forgotten.

Pests and diseases

It would be repetitious to keep stating that no particular pests attack each of the plants described, so a general note is included here to mention one or two. Greenfly, and aphids in general, can be a nuisance, particularly after a mild winter; there are several effective sprays on the market to deal with them. At least greenfly can be seen with comparative ease, but the hidden pest chewing away at the underground parts of a plant is difficult to trace and to eradicate. One such is the vine weevil larva, which eat roots – particularly those of primulas; the first indication of its presence is the sudden deterioration of the plants. On investigation, the grubs will be found in the soil; aldrin or lindane dust will control this pest, which may attack other plants if in pots in a greenhouse. Root aphids sometimes attack the European primulas, such as *P. auricula,* and malathion is the control here. Otherwise, apart from slugs perhaps, it can be said that alpines are comparatively pest- and disease-free.

Expanding the interest

Rock gardening is almost a disease, for if it gets hold of you there is no cure! As your enthusiasm increases, you will want to propagate plants – not only to replenish any gaps in your garden, but to exchange with others. There is nothing more pleasant for the visitor than to depart with a handful of plants. You may then wish to progress to an alpine house, where the treasures of the high mountains can be housed. When you are really hooked, there is the possibility of exhibiting at one of the specialist societies' shows.

In this short introduction it is possible to mention only a few points, but one final remark must be made about bulbs on the rock garden. They are absolutely invaluable and can provide a colourful show from the early aconites to the late-flowering crocuses; do not overlook their tremendous potential. Dwarf tulips and narcissi are particularly useful in spring, with the dwarf cyclamen helping through into late summer.

All this has touched only very lightly on a vast subject. I hope you are inspired to continue your interest.

Above: **Achillea tomentosa**
The flat yellow flowerheads of this miniature yarrow make a colourful splash in summer. 17♦

Above left: **Acaena buchananii**
The New Zealand burrs make excellent ground cover plants and have an interesting range of foliage colours. Spiny fruits in autumn. 17♦

Left: **Aethionema 'Warley Ruber'**
This plant makes a brilliant display in early summer but needs to be kept going by cuttings each year. 18♦

Below: **Allium narcissiflorum**
One of the many dwarf onions. It will thrive in a sunny spot. 19♦

13

Above:
Alyssum saxatile 'Citrinum'
The pale lemon-yellow form is not as vigorous as the type, but still needs plenty of room to spread. 19♦

Below:
Androsace primuloides 'Chumbyi'
One of the easiest of the Himalayan rock jasmines for spring flowers. 21♦

Above: **Alyssum saxatile
'Dudley Neville'**
This vigorous plant is at its best *cascading down a wall. The beautiful biscuit-coloured flowers appear during the spring.* 20♦

Above: **Antennaria dioica 'Rosea'**
The pink flowers of catsfoot blend well with the grey foliage to make a useful carpet in paving as well as in the rock garden. It thrives in full sunshine and well-draining soil. 22♦

Below:
Anemone blanda 'Atrocaerulea'
The seedlings of this bulb are attractively variable, but this dark blue form is one of the most beautiful in early spring. 22♦

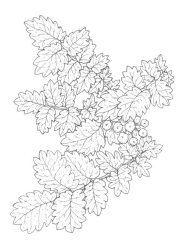

Acaena buchananii
- **Full sun**
- **Any soil**
- **Ground cover**

This is one of a large family of plants, mainly native to New Zealand, which are useful subjects for ground cover and under-planting with dwarf bulbs. They are admittedly invasive, but excellent for a poor soil and a hot dry sunny position. They are grown mainly for foliage, but the spiny seed heads are attractive in their own right. *A. buchananii* has grey-green foliage with yellowish brown burrs. The flowers are insignificant and the leaves small, neat and briar-like in appearance, making a mat no higher than 5cm (2in) tall.

Propagation is simple, by dividing the runners in autumn or spring, making sure there is a good root system to each runner.

Achillea tomentosa
- **Full sun**
- **Poor soil**
- **Evergreen**

This carpeting plant grows throughout SW Europe across to central Italy, thriving in full sun on a starvation diet. It is particularly suitable for growing in crevices and dry walls. There are several species in the wild, but most have flowers that are too weedy and unattractive. *A. tomentosa* is the most popular alpine yarrow in gardens, with softly hairy and ferny grey leaves forming prostrate mats from which arise the flat yellow 4cm (1.6in) wide flowerheads on 15cm (6in) stems.

Slugs seem to be partial to the foliage in spring, but metaldehyde pellets placed around it will deter them.

Propagation is by soft cuttings in a sand frame between midsummer and early autumn, or by division in spring. Autumn divisions should be kept in a frame over winter.

Take care
This is not a plant for a damp situation, but it does very well in the cracks of paving stones. 12♦

Take care
Never give this plant a rich diet: kindness will kill it. 13♦

Aethionema 'Warley Ruber'

- Full sun
- Any well-drained soil
- Evergreen sub-shrub

The shrubby aethionemas give of their best in a hot dry situation on the rock garden. They thrive on sunny limestone in the Mediterranean region, but in cultivation will tolerate a neutral soil. They form neat plants of bushy habit with blue-grey leaves, and the small pink flowers are borne in clusters at the end of the branches. 'Warley Ruber' makes a plant about 15cm (6in) tall.

Removal of the flowering stems is not only a neat practice but assists with the propagation of the plant, as the non-flowering soft growth thus created is ideal for taking cuttings from midsummer onwards. Insert in a sand frame and pot up as soon as roots form. When established they should be pinched out and will then be ready for planting out in the spring.

Take care
Do not plant on an acid soil. 12♦

Alchemilla erythropoda

- Full sun
- Any soil
- Herbaceous

This is a miniature of that marvellous frothy green-flowered weed, *A. mollis* (Ladies' Mantle), which seeds itself about gardens in a prolific manner and is much beloved by flower arrangers. *A. erythropoda* is a native of the Balkans, but does well in most situations, tolerating a variety of soils and conditions. Its greeny flowers come in early to mid-summer and sometimes have a reddish tinge in the flowerhead, which is no more than 10cm (4in) tall, although some references indicate it could reach 30cm (12in), possibly in a rich soil.

Propagation is by division in spring, planting out directly or potting up. Although other alchemillas are invasive, *A. erythropoda* can be classified as well-behaved.

Take care
To keep it dwarf and discourage any tendency to spread, plant in a poorish soil.

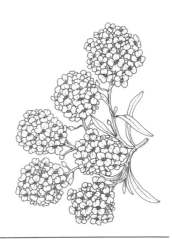

Allium narcissiflorum
- Sunny position
- Well-drained soil
- Bulbous

Alyssum saxatile 'Citrinum'
- Sunny position
- Any well-drained soil
- Evergreen sub-shrub

The onion family is widespread throughout the Northern Hemisphere and contains some species that are blatantly rampant and should never be allowed near a garden, but *A. narcissiflorum* – one of the many dwarf species – is well behaved. Found wild in Northern Italy and Southern France it grows happily in screes, which suggests that it requires free drainage in the garden. It has a wide tolerance of varying soil conditions, and it flowers in midsummer, producing on its 15-35cm (6-14in) flower stem an umbel of bell-shaped flowers of purple-pink hues. It is one of the most attractive of the small onions and does well in a sunny position.

Propagation is simple: collect the seed in autumn and sow it in late winter, and young seedlings will be ready in late spring for autumn planting.

A. saxatile itself is a much maligned plant, along with *Iberis* and *Aubrieta*, but it must be admitted that all three have been over-planted in the past. However, *A. saxatile* certainly provides a magnificent splash of colour with its bright golden-yellow flowers in spring. This brilliant display is all the more encouraged if the plant is cut back hard after flowering. It enjoys a sunny spot, particularly on the top of a dry wall, and is not fussy about its diet, preferring poorer soil. It does well when it can be unrestrained and can mingle with other vigorous rock plants (such as campanulas and pinks) to give a continuous display. 'Citrinum' has pale lemon-yellow flowers.

For propagation, see *A. saxatile* 'Dudley Neville'.

Take care
Ensure this plant has a well-drained site. 13♦

Take care
This is not a plant for shade or woodland. 14♦

Alyssum saxatile 'Dudley Neville'
- Sunny position
- Any well-drained soil
- Evergreen sub-shrub

Anacyclus depressus
(Mount Atlas daisy)
- Sunny scree
- Well-drained site
- Evergreen

The parent plant, *A. saxatile*, can be 20-30cm (8-12in) tall, but the named cultivars tend to be slightly less vigorous. These include 'Compactum', which lives up to its name at 15cm (6in); 'Plenum', with double flowers; 'Citrinum', with lemon-yellow flowers; and 'Dudley Neville', with unusual biscuit-coloured flowers that are comparatively restrained when set against their brilliant relatives.

Propagation of the parent species is easy from seed. Sow in late summer and pot on in autumn, and young plants are available for the following spring. The named cultivars cannot be guaranteed to come true from seed; they should be increased from cuttings, taken in mid- to late summer and inserted in a sand frame. Pot up in autumn, pinching out the centres to encourage a bushy plant.

This attractive plant comes from the Atlas Mountains in Morocco, which might suggest that it is not over-hardy. However, it survives all but the most severe winters and forms a neat mat of grey-green ferny foliage that lies prostrate on the soil; one plant can make a 30cm (12in) spread. The flowers are no more than 5cm (2in) tall and can be 5cm (2in) across. Their attraction lies in the pinky-maroon backing to the petals in bud, but the wide open daisy-like flowers are pure white.

Ideally *A. depressus* should be planted in a well-drained situation in full sun. Cover with glass in winter.

Propagation is by seed, gathered carefully by placing a sheet of paper under the seedhead when it is quite dry, and shaking them onto the paper. Sow fresh seed in the autumn in a gritty mixture at 8-10°C (45-50°F). Failing this, sow in late winter, freeze for a night or two and bring into the same temperature.

Take care
This is a plant for a sunny spot. 15▶

Take care
Never keep in wet conditions.

Andromeda polifolia 'Compacta'
- Semi-shade
- Leaf-mould or peaty soil
- Evergreen

The type species is a native of the wet bogs of Central and Northern Europe, including Great Britain. It tends to be straggly, producing stems 15-35cm (6-14in) long. The small leaves are dark green above, and silver below; the small (5mm/0.2in) pink flowers are produced in the axils of the leaves at the tips of the stems in early summer. The flower stalks are whitish and the whole flower fades to white. However, because of its neater habit, it is better to cultivate the form 'Compacta', whose name is descriptive of its behaviour. It is of Japanese origin. In cultivation this plant is happy in a dampish situation in the peat garden.

Propagation takes a long time: cuttings of non-flowering wood, inserted in a shaded peat frame, can take up to 12 months to reach sufficient size to plant out.

Take care
Do not plant in a dry place.

Androsace primuloides 'Chumbyi'
(Rock jasmine)
- Open situation
- Any soil
- Evergreen

This family evokes a response from every keen gardener, when he espies the neat domes covered in intense white flowers. Alas, these are not for the garden, but for the alpine house and special culture. *A. primuloides (sarmentosa)* from the Himalaya provides us with a number of varieties that are suitable for the rock garden. The plants form rosettes 3-5cm (1.25-2in) across and these form mats some 60cm (2ft) across. The pink flowerheads reach no taller than 10cm (4in). 'Chumbyi' is more compact and of more robust constitution.

The well-drained soil should contain some humus. Winter wetness affects the rosettes, so some protection is advisable.

Propagation is by potting up rooted rosettes in early autumn, which will be ready for planting out the following spring after over-wintering under protection.

Take care
Protect from birds; the soft rosettes are lovely for nests. 14♦

21

Anemone blanda 'Atrocaerulea'

(Windflower)
- Cool position
- Leafy soil
- Herbaceous bulb

This popular anemone is from SE Europe and Turkey. Its tuberous rhizomes produce fleshy leaves divided into three or more leaflets. It is a useful plant because it flowers at a time of year when colour is thin in the garden – from winter into early spring. The flowers are a good blue, star-shaped and 2-4cm (0.8-1.6in) across, on stems up to 15cm (6in).

This species thrives in a cool or semi-shaded position in any soil that has good drainage; this can be on the rock garden under the shelter of a rock. The rhizomes are available commercially in late summer for early autumn planting at a depth of 4-5cm (1.5-2in). Mark its position because leaves die down after flowering.

Seed takes two years or more to germinate, after sowing in midsummer when it is fresh. An alternative method is to divide the small rhizomes in midsummer.

Take care
Plant the rhizomes where they can be seen from the house in winter. 16♦

Antennaria dioica 'Rosea'

- Any situation
- Any well-drained soil
- Evergreen

A useful carpeting plant that forms a prostrate mat up to 45cm (18in) across of pointed silvery leaves with short flower stems, 5-10cm (2-4in), producing rich pink flowers. Antennarias are found in Europe, Asia and North America, where one bears the hideous name of 'Rosy Pussy Paws' – actually quite an apt description of the flowers.

'Rosea' is useful on any well-drained soil, the height of the flower varying according to the richness of the situation, but it does especially well in paving or on the edge of a path. Bulbs can be planted under it and it is a useful subject for an alpine lawn.

Propagation is by division in spring or late summer, planted out direct or potted up. It is a tough plant that does not succumb to pests or diseases.

Take care
Be sure to give first-class drainage. 16♦

Anthyllis montana

(Mountain kidney vetch)
- Hot situation in full sunshine
- Well-drained dry soil
- Evergreen

The pea family forms a huge collection – some utterly weedy, others quite attractive. Most are happy in any garden soil and some are useful on the rock garden. Of those suitable for gardens, *A. montana* is the best, forming a small woody bush up to 30cm (12in) tall. The hairy foliage gives a silvery appearance and the flowers are red or red-purple, produced at the stem ends.

Although it comes from the Alps and mountain regions of southern Europe, this species is best planted in a sunny spot in a very well-drained gritty soil. It tolerates limestone.

Propagation is by cuttings taken with a heel in summer and inserted in a sand frame. Seed is rarely set, but can be sown in early spring. The plant produces a tap-root that resents disturbance and so once planted it should not be moved. It has no pests or diseases that plague it.

Take care
Not a plant for a damp acid soil. 33♦

Aquilegia scopulorum
- Sunny position
- Well-drained soil
- Herbaceous

Border species of columbines have an attractive range of flowers in pastel shades, but produce hundreds of seedlings that are difficult to eradicate. Beware also of packets of so-called 'alpine aquilegias' that turn out to be 60cm (24in) tall horrors. Strangely, the true alpine species are easy to grow, although they have a reputation for being short-lived, perhaps because the conditions they enjoy in nature cannot be emulated in cultivation. *A. scopulorum* comes from the Rocky Mountains, and to retain its dwarf (10cm/4in) habit, it should be given the starvation diet of a stony scree. Its 4cm (1.6in) long flowers are produced on 7-8cm (2.75-3.2in) stems from mid- to late summer, and face upwards. The colour is from pale lavender to deep violet and the leaves are a delightful grey-green.

Propagation is by seed sown in late winter at 8°C (45°F). Prick out and harden off.

Take care
Gather seed from isolated plants.

Arabis ferdinandi-coburgii 'Variegata'
- Full or partial sunshine
- Any soil
- Evergreen

The better known *A. albida* is really too invasive to be included in any list of rock plants; its white flowers appear fleetingly in spring and leave a not-too-tidy plant for the rest of the year, though in its favour it must be said that it is admirable for a dry stony bank. So it is to *A. ferdinandi-coburgii* 'Variegata' that we turn for its conspicuous variegated foliage. It forms a tight mat up to 30cm (12in) across that is so attractive as to warrant the removal of the short white flowers borne on 8cm (3.2in) stems. Unlike some plants, it retains its bright variegation throughout the year.

Propagation is by division at almost any time, but it is best in late autumn or early spring. Cuttings can be taken with a heel, or some old wood at the base, in late summer.

This relative of the cabbage sometimes suffers from the same pests and diseases.

Take care
To retain the best variegation, do not give too rich a diet.

Arenaria balearica
(Sandwort)
- Moist shady situation
- Peaty soil
- Evergreen

A quietly attractive plant that forms a prostrate mat of tiny green leaves, with masses of single white flowers on 2-3cm (0.8-1.25in) stems.

It requires a damp situation and will grow attractively over the face of a damp porous rock or peat block. I have found it difficult to establish, but once it does settle, it will stay. It is an unobtrusive plant, easy to eradicate if it becomes invasive; and although it spreads, it does so gently and with no harm to the plants it overruns. It comes from the Balearics and other Mediterranean islands; it can be seen in complete shade between rocks at sea level in Sardinia.

Propagation is by division in early autumn, planting direct. It dislikes being potted up, but this can be overcome by plunging a plant in peat and taking the pieces as they root.

Take care
This plant does not take kindly to direct exposure to sunshine. 33♦

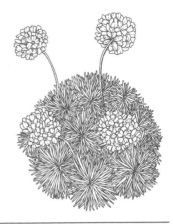

Arisarum proboscideum
(Mousetail plant)
● **Shady situation**
● **Leafy soil**
● **Deciduous**

This is a curious little plant for a shady site in the peat garden or a northern aspect, where it will spread inoffensively. It is of great attraction to children, as the 8-10cm (3.2-4in) 'tails' at the end of the flower look like so many mice disappearing into the forest of arrow-shaped leaves. Dismissed by some as a curiosity, it is not one of nature's most brightly coloured products, but its quiet charm is attractive to the discerning gardener. The flower, which appears in spring, is technically a spathe, which is inflated and terminates in the 'tail'. It is olive green above and white beneath, with occasional dull purple striping. It is a native of central Italy and SW Spain.

Propagation is simple by division in late spring, after flowering; pot up in a peaty or leaf-mould compost. The leaves tend to die down or turn brown in late summer, so it should not be thought that the plant is dying.

Take care
This plant does not like full sun.

Armeria juniperifolia 'Bevan's Variety'
(Thrift)
● **Open situation**
● **Well-drained soil**
● **Evergreen**

A. juniperifolia, from Spain, will still be found catalogued as *A. caespitosa*, the name by which it was originally known until a recent re-classification. It has long been a popular rock garden plant, producing a neat 5-7cm (2-2.75in) high tussock of narrow dark green leaves, from which emerge in spring short-stemmed heads of pink flowers. In fact the flowers are almost stemless, a fact that is emphasized in the form 'Bevan's Variety' where the deep rose flowerheads almost nestle in the bed of needle-like leaves. It does extremely well in sunny places.

Seed rarely comes true, particularly if other thrifts are in the garden, so it is best to take small cuttings in summer, with about 7mm (0.25in) of old brown wood at the base. Insert in a cutting compost and pot on in gritty soil.

It tolerates lime and has no pests to trouble it; rarely, the leaves are attacked by a rust in spring.

Take care
Give good drainage and full sun. 34●

Armeria maritima 'Bloodstone'

(Sea pink)
- **Open situation**
- **Any good garden soil**
- **Evergreen**

A. maritima is a native of most of Europe, where it can be found from sea level in Britain to the high mountains of central Europe. It has many sub-species and forms and some of the latter have been selected for garden cultivation; 'Bloodstone' is one such. Although its 20-25cm (8-10in) dark red flowers are an attractive colour, care should be taken in placing this plant in the small rock garden, as it is really for the larger rock garden or the front of a border, where it looks more in proportion.

It will do well in a sunny spot, but will tolerate a partially shaded position more than other thrifts.

Propagation is by 7-8cm (2.75-3.2in) long cuttings, with some old wood at the base, inserted in a sand frame in summer. They can be divided in early spring, but this sometimes results in untidy plants.

Take care
Do not overfeed this plant, or it may become lanky and out of character. 34↓

Artemisia stellerana 'Mori's Form'

- **Full sun**
- **Any well-drained soil**
- **Herbaceous**

This whole genus is attractive for its aromatic grey foliage. *A. stellerana* itself comes from North America and Eastern Asia, and in Japan a nurseryman selected his own form: 'Mori's Form'. This reaches a maximum of 15cm (6in) and produces deeply lobed grey leaves, not dissimilar to a chrysanthemum leaf, which are almost white; in late summer, there appear panicles of yellowish daisy flowers, but these are of no great attraction compared to the foliage.

This species needs to be planted in full sun to give of its best, and a poor soil would suit it, although it is quite accommodating.

Propagation is by cuttings taken in mid- to late summer and inserted in a sand frame. They root very quickly and are ready to pot up within a month, or to plant out the following spring.

Take care
Do not put this plant in a shaded, damp position. 35↓

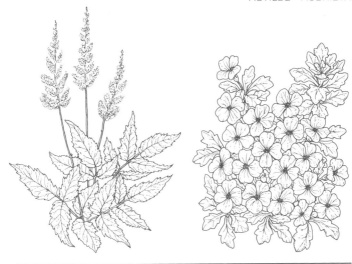

Astilbe chinensis 'Pumila'

- Moist shady situation
- Leafy soil
- Herbaceous

Aubrieta 'Ballawley Amethyst'

- Open situation
- Any well-drained soil
- Evergreen

The mention of *Astilbe* may conjure up in the mind visions of the 1m (39in) tall spikes of pink and dark red flowers found growing in wet spots by the side of ponds and streams in spring. The dwarf species are no less attractive, and are useful for filling in the gap between spring and autumn, for they flower in summer through to early autumn.

A. chinensis 'Pumila' produces a 23cm (9in) tall narrow spike of deep pink flowers, slightly flushed with purple, from a base of fern-like leaves. It requires a cool spot, perhaps at the base of a rock where its roots can shelter. Full sun can be tolerated provided there is ample water in summer.

Propagation is by division in spring, taking care not to split the plants into too small units. The new young plants will certainly need moisture and a shady position while establishing, and should do well in a leafy or peaty soil.

Take care
Never let this plant dry out. 36♦

Aubrietas are almost too well known to need description. There are a number of species but the best garden plants come from selected seedlings of *A. deltoidea*, which occurs naturally throughout southern Europe from Sicily to Asia Minor. Cultivation is easy provided you can give it the dry conditions on a sunny bank or dry wall that it requires. It thrives on chalk or in alkaline conditions, where it gives of its best with a colourful spring display. There are many named forms, in colours ranging from pale pink through to blue and violet-blue.

To encourage neat plants, cut the dead flowerheads off with shears, and by late summer the new growth should have covered up any untidiness. The plants form mats up to 60cm (2ft) wide and the flower-heads are 8-10cm (3.2-4in) tall.

Propagation is by division in early autumn. The parent plant, or part of it, is taken to pieces and potted up.

Take care
Add lime to the soil if it is acid. 37♦

Azorella trifurcata

- **Open situation but not direct sunshine**
- **Good drainage but with moisture**
- **Evergreen**

This is a rather confused plant, which has suffered from a name change and so may be found as *Bolax glebaria* in catalogues. What is not in doubt is its habitat in South America, where it is native to the Falkland Islands and Chile.

It forms a spreading symmetrical mat on a stony sunny scree, which should have a degree of moisture about, or it can usefully be employed in the alpine house. The hummocks are composed of rosettes of leathery green leaves, and might make a spread of up to 90cm (3ft), but be only 7-8cm (2.75-3.2in) tall. The flowers are minute and yellow, appearing in midsummer on short stems. The main claim to fame for this plant is its neat symmetry.

It spreads slowly, and this provides the method of propagation, as the spreading stems root as they go. Remove some rosettes in spring for propagation, and for neatness.

Take care
Do not expect a brilliant floral display from this particular plant. 37♦

Campanula cochlearifolia

(Fairies' thimbles)
- **Any situation**
- **Any soil**
- **Evergreen**

To choose just two examples from this huge genus is an unkindness, when there are so many that are such garden-worthy plants. However, *C. cochlearifolia* (sometimes still listed as *C. pusilla*) is so good-tempered as to be suitable for most soils and situations. It is native to the European Alps, where it thrives on and around limestone rocks and is happiest in stony ground where it can run freely. Thus in cultivation it enjoys scree conditions where its blue bells can push their way up on 5-8cm (2-3.2in) stems from the heart-shaped basal leaves. Although it spreads it can be controlled very easily, but it is attractive enough to deter such a move. There are forms ranging from white to deep blue.

Propagation is by division between early autumn and spring, or by soft cuttings in late spring or early autumn.

Take care
This is not an invasive plant, but give it space to roam. 38♦

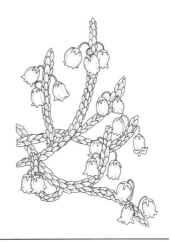

Campanula poscharskyana

- **Sunny situation**
- **Not too rich a soil**
- **Evergreen**

This species has been described as 'rampageous but lovely', which conveys the necessary warning for this attractive invader. The plant forms a tangled mat of roots and stems that is difficult to eradicate. Thus it is best planted where it can be confined or in a corner where nothing else will do well. It is ideal for a dry wall or an area of poor soil, where it will produce dozens of its clear lavender-blue bell-shaped flowers on 30cm (12in) stems. These flowers totally obscure the sharply toothed rounded leaves. The spread of one plant can be as much as 60-90cm (2-3ft).

An allied plant, only one degree less invasive, is *C. portenschlagiana*, which has the additional advantage of flowering well in shady conditions.

Propagation is obviously no problem. Divide the plant, probably with a spade, in autumn or spring.

Take care
Make sure that this attractive plant is starved, and not planted near more precious subjects.

Cassiope lycopodioides

- **Semi-shade**
- **Acid soil**
- **Evergreen shrub**

Masses of wiry evergreen stems, with no leaves apparent (as they are adpressed to the stems), form a flat mat of green with an optimum spread of 50cm (20in). From this green carpet in mid- to late spring are produced small pure white 5-6mm (0.2-0.25in) bells with red calyces. These appear just above the foliage and in a good form almost obscure it.

This is a plant for a cool spot in the rock garden with dappled shade, and is ideal for the peat garden, where it will quickly make itself at home. It comes from NE Asia, along with several other species that vary in size and height. There are also one or two named cultivars of *C. lycopodioides*.

Propagation is by young soft cuttings taken in midsummer, with or without a heel; insert them in a peat and sand frame, where they must not dry out. Rooting is slow, but pot on the young rooted plants in autumn; over-winter in a cold frame.

Take care
This plant dislikes lime and hot sun.

Ceratostigma plumbaginoides

- **Any open situation**
- **Any soil**
- **Herbaceous**

This Chinese species is one of the beauties of the garden in autumn, when other plants are dying down. Its red-tinged foliage deepens as autumn proceeds and its 2cm (0.8in) wide terminal cluster of blue flowers arrives from late summer onwards. The plant is completely hardy and unharmed by early frosts, although some say otherwise. It can spread to about 40cm (16in), but cannot be considered invasive, although its roots install themselves fairly firmly.

This is an accommodating plant, but will thrive better in a well-drained warmish spot where it will reach its full height of 30cm (12in). Some purists would banish it from the rock garden, but its unarguable case would be the usefulness of both leaf and flower in the autumn.

Propagation is simply by division in spring, just before growth begins. Division in autumn would spoil the plant at its peak.

Take care
Do not plant in a damp situation. 38♦

Chionodoxa luciliae

(Glory of the snow)
- **Needs some sunshine**
- **Requires a good soil**
- **Deciduous bulb**

This bulb, from the mountains of western Turkey, is cultivated with ease in Britain and America, but seems to succeed in the Southern Hemisphere only when it is planted deeply in a cool shady spot. The 15-20cm (6-8in) stems carry up to ten flowers in a one-sided raceme. The flowers are lilac-blue, 2-2.5cm (0.8-1in) wide, with a white centre and yellow anthers; they appear in late winter and early spring, which is a useful time for flowers. They naturalize freely in the garden, increasing by both seed and the production of bulbils.

A sunny, well-drained position is ideal, but I have seen this bulb naturalized under deciduous shrubs, producing a carpet of blue.

Seed can be sown when fresh, either in the ground or in a pot. They should be left until the foliage dies down the following year before transplanting.

Take care
Never plant these bulbs in ground that is likely to be disturbed. 39♦

Convolvulus mauritanicus
- Sheltered sunny situation
- Light dry soil
- Herbaceous

A cautious look spreads across the faces of inexperienced gardeners if this relative of the invasive bindweed is recommended. However, whereas bindweed is a tough customer, there is a degree of tenderness among some of its Mediterranean relatives.

C. mauritanicus comes from North Africa and benefits from being planted in a warm sunny corner, where some protection can be added in winter. It is spreading, with trailing stems up to 60cm (2ft) long, which produce a succession of clear blue, white-throated trumpet flowers in late summer and early autumn.

Seed can be sown in spring, but a good method of keeping the plant over the winter is by taking cuttings of non-flowering wood in summer and keeping them under glass in heat, stopping the rooted plants to ensure a good growth for the following year.

Take care
This plant would not be happy in a cold, wet situation. 39▶

Corydalis cheilanthifolia
- Prefers some sunshine
- Any soil
- Herbaceous

The most desirable of this genus is the blue *Corydalis cashmiriana* from Kashmir, but it is not freely available, partly because of its fickle behaviour in dying out for no apparent reason. So we have to make do with *C. cheilanthifolia* from China, with ferny leaves and bright yellow flowers. It is a worthwhile plant, surviving well and seeding about unobtrusively in almost any soil. It tolerates more sun than most of the species, and the foliage takes on a bronzy hue when it has plenty of light. The flower spikes make the plant about 20cm (8in) tall.

Propagation is by seed sown in late winter, or by seeking out self-sown seedlings in the garden. It is essential to sow seed thinly and to handle the seedlings before the main tap-root is formed. Young plants do not like staying in a pot too long.

Take care
Put this plant where there is room for it to seed about.

Crocus speciosus

(Autumn crocus)
- **Sunny situation**
- **Well-drained soil**
- **Bulbous**

Cyclamen coum

- **Semi-shade**
- **Well-drained soil**
- **Deciduous corm**

The spring crocuses are well-known enough to be mentioned in passing. The large Dutch crocuses do not lend themselves to the scale of the smaller rock garden. The smaller, late-winter flowering varieties of *C. chrysanthus* provide splendid splashes of colour to suit all tastes, from the brashness of 'Zwanenburg Bronze' in orange and yellow, to the delicate creamy 'Snow Bunting'.

C. speciosus comes from SE Europe, Asia and Iran. Its 10-12cm (4-4.75in) lilac-blue flowers have the added attraction of yellow anthers and scarlet stigmas. In the variety 'Aitchisonii' the larger flowers have attractive veining.

C. speciosus naturalizes well. Propagation is variable by seed, so the corms should be lifted and the smaller ones grown on.

If you are not too pedantic it is fun to raise plants of this species from seed, for you will find there is a tremendous variation. To some, that is the attraction of this winter-flowering species. The leaves are round or kidney-shaped, and can be entirely green or marbled with silver. The flower colours vary from dark magenta or crimson through to rose-pink and pure white, the latter still retaining the red or purple blotch at the base of the petals. The flowers look more square than other cyclamen and are about 2cm (0.8in) in size on 7-8cm (2.75-3.2in) stems. They naturalize well under trees and shrubs, and look good in a cool situation on the rock garden, where they benefit from a top-dressing of bonemeal once a year.

Propagation is by seed as soon as the capsules are ripe.

Take care
Do not plant in a waterlogged situation.

Take care
Mark where this plant is growing, to avoid disturbing it in summer.

Above: **Anthyllis montana**
*This easily grown European alpine
needs full sun to give of its best
throughout the summer.* 23♦

Below: **Arenaria balearica**
*May be difficult to establish, but once
settled in it will spread gently to cover
rock faces. Grow in shade.* 24♦

Above: **Armeria juniperifolia 'Bevan's Variety'**
A neat little tuft of grass-like leaves produces short flowers in early summer. It is dwarf enough to be planted in a trough or sink. 25♦

Left:
Armeria maritima 'Bloodstone'
Perhaps more suitable for the larger rock garden, this cultivar is quite tall at 20cm (8in). One of the more vigorous cultivars. 26♦

Right:
Artemisia stellarana 'Mori's form'
One of the more spectacular foliage plants for the rock garden with first-class grey foliage; the flowers are of no account. 26♦

Above: **Astilbe chinensis 'Pumila'**
Most astilbes like to grow by the side of water, but this dwarf form tolerates *drier conditions and produces its pink spikes quite readily in late summer.* 27♦

Above:
Aubrieta 'Ballawley Amethyst'
The popular aubrietas can be relied on for colour in spring. 27♦

Below: **Azorella trifurcata**
Sometimes catalogued under Bolax, *it has a confused history, but forms a neat and attractive cushion.* 28♦

Above: **Campanula cochlearifolia**
These flowers are a delight when seen in the wild, and look equally attractive in cultivation. 28♦

Right: **Chionodoxa luciliae**
A colourful early-flowering bulb that is extremely hardy and spreads to make an attractive display. 30♦

Below left:
Ceratostigma plumbaginoides
A useful autumn-flowering plant that has red tinted foliage. 30♦

Below right:
Convolvulus mauritanicus
Although related to the bindweed, it has less invasive tendencies. 31♦

Left: Cyclamen hederifolium
Formerly known as C. neapolitanum this produces its flowers during late summer, which is a useful time of year on the rock garden. It is very easily raised from seed. 49♦

Right: Cytisus × beanii
This dwarf broom is useful for planting above a rock or as illustrated on a dry wall, where it can tumble down colourfully. 49♦

Below: Daphne cneorum
One of the most delightfully scented of all alpines, this dwarf shrub has quite a spreading habit, but it can be forgiven because it is such good value. Grow in the open. 50♦

Above: **Dianthus neglectus**
One of the gems of the large family of pinks, which all thrive on alkaline soils and give such good displays in early summer. 50♦

Below: **Diascia cordata**
The terracotta-pink flowers come during summer. This plant definitely requires a warm situation that is not too exposed. 51♦

Above: **Dodecatheon pauciflora**
*There is some doubt about this
name, for it sometimes appears as*
D.meadia. *Whatever their botanical
name, however, these American
plants enjoy a moist situation.* 52♦

Left: **Dryas octopetala**
A native of Europe and America, this plant produces creamy white flowers in spring; these are then followed by attractive fluffy seedheads. 52♦

Right: **Epimedium alpinum**
This is a useful foliage plant with unusual flowers that are generally to be found hidden away. 53♦

Below left: **Edraianthus pumilio**
A plant for the well-drained scree or trough, where it will flower as illustrated. 53♦

Below right: **Eranthis hyemalis**
The winter aconite is one of the first bulbs to appear in late winter. It is not always easy to establish, but keen gardeners should persevere. 54♦

Above: **Erinus alpinus**
One of Nature's accommodating plants that seeds itself about the garden happily and unobtrusively to give a colourful display in early summer. 55♦

Left: **Erigeron mucronatus**
Another plant that will seed about, and it is at its best in the cracks between paving stones. It is an attractive little daisy with lovely pink flowers during summer. 54♦

Right: **Erysimum 'Jubilee Gold'**
The dwarf wallflowers make a splash in spring, producing their colourful rich yellow flowers from chocolate-coloured buds. 55♦

Above: **Erythronium 'Pagoda'**
*One of a number of useful bulbs from
North America that prefer a cooler
site in the garden.* 56♦

Below: **Euryops acraeus**
Formerly known as E.evansii, *this
dwarf shrub from South Africa has
proved hardy in cultivation.* 57♦

Cyclamen hederifolium

(Sowbread)
- Semi-shaded site
- Peaty or leafy soil
- Corm

Cytisus × beanii
- Sunny situation
- Light soil
- Deciduous shrub

This may be better-known as *C. neapolitanum*, though it comes from Italy through to western Turkey. It is freely available as a dried corm, but this may take a time to establish itself, so it is best to purchase the plant in growth. The genus can provide several species to give a succession of flower throughout the year. *C. hederifolium* appears in late summer and its flowers are a miniature version (2.5cm/1in) of the larger pot plants seen in florists'. The leaves are ivy-shaped and have decorative marbling. The plants can seed about, given semi-shade and leaf-mould. A pure white form is also in cultivation, but the pink is prettier.

Propagation is by seed and there is some variation. Fresh seed should be sown in a peat-based seed compost and kept moist. Alternatively, young self-sown seedlings can be potted up. Slugs are partial to young seedlings.

This is a semi-prostrate hybrid shrub, with a spread of 60cm (2ft). It is essential for the larger rock garden, where it can spread to its full 90cm (3ft). The 12mm (0.5in) long yellow pea-like flowers are borne in late spring or early summer along the previous year's growths.

This is a hybrid of garden origin and like most members of the pea family it is a sun-loving plant that grows easily in any well-drained soil.

Propagation is by taking cuttings, with or without a heel, in early summer, selecting shoots that are beginning to harden, and a minimum of 5cm (2in) long. Insert in a sandy frame and when potting on take care not to damage the roots. None of this family likes transplanting, so once planted out, *C. × beanii* should never be disturbed. It is good in alkaline conditions.

Take care
Protect the corms from mice by covering with wire netting. 40♦

Take care
Never plant this shrub in a wet situation. 41♦

Daphne cneorum

(Garland flower)
- Fairly open situation
- Well-drained loam with lime
- Evergreen

This plant of the central and southern European hills seems to do better in cultivation than in the wild, where it often appears scrappy. It is highly scented, and therefore of double value in a garden. Officially it makes a mat 90cm (3ft) across, but I have seen one at least 1.5m (5ft) across in a chalky garden. The many twiggy branches produce clusters of fragrant rosy flowers in spring and possibly again in autumn. It does well in any soil, but benefits from a top-dressing of leaf-mould each year to cover the bare stems.

Propagation is a tease. Cuttings of non-flowering shoots taken in midsummer, dipped in rooting hormone and inserted in a shaded peat frame, have always had a high incidence of losses. Another way is to work sand and peat down between the branches in late spring to encourage them to layer, and then to remove the rooted layers for over-wintering in a cold frame.

Take care
Never move this plant once it is established. 40-41♦

Dianthus neglectus

(D. pavonius)
- Open situation
- Lime-free soil
- Evergreen

Pinks usually thrive on alkaline soils, but this is an exception, as it is to be found on lime-free soils in the eastern and southern European Alps. It forms a neat hummock of grey-green linear leaves that varies in height from 10-20cm (4-8in). It must be admitted that the flowers are variable, and so a good form must be chosen; the flowers are from pale pink to deep crimson, but always with a distinctive buff reverse. At best they are 3cm (1.25in) across, on short stems that hold them just above the foliage, in midsummer.

This species does well in a sunny spot in well-drained soil, but appreciates being moist in summer and less so in winter.

Propagation is by soft cuttings taken in midsummer from non-flowering shoots and inserted in a sandy cutting frame. The plants will be ready by late winter.

Take care
Do not plant in chalky or alkaline conditions. 42♦

Dianthus nitidus

- Open situation
- Leafy soil, gritty, with lime
- Evergreen

This is a lime-loving plant from the Carpathian Mountains of Czechoslovakia and Poland, similar to *D. alpinus*, but taller. It is distinguished by its bright green leaves rather than the grey ones normal to the genus. The 2.5cm (1in) wide purple-red flowers are carried above the leaves on a flower stem up to 10cm (4in) long, from early to late summer. The flower buds are almost black. Unfortunately, the true plant is not always to be found in commerce, and inferior forms are in circulation.

This plant appreciates a loamy, leafy soil but with the addition of some lime; as it requires good drainage, limestone chippings could be used to good effect.

Propagation from seed merely assists the production of poor forms, so it is best increased in the same manner as *D. neglectus*, by soft cuttings in midsummer.

Take care
Provide good drainage and some lime for best results.

Diascia cordata

- Warm open situation
- Well-drained soil
- Evergreen

Plants from South Africa are usually suspect for hardiness, but this plant has seemed hardy now for some years. Perhaps its habitat at 2,500m (8,200ft) in the Drakensberg Mountains has built up its resistance to winter cold. It is an attractive plant, producing 15-25cm (6-10in) long racemes of pinky terracotta flowers, 1.5cm (0.6in) wide, from a dense mat of leafy stems that are more or less prostrate.

It relishes a warm position in any well-drained soil, where it will flower in summer.

Propagation is by cuttings of young shoots taken in summer and placed in a sand frame. When rooted these should be over-wintered in a frame before planting out the following spring.

Take care
Make sure this plant is not placed in an exposed situation. 42

Dodecatheon meadia

(Shooting star)
● **Damp situation**
● **Leafy soil**
● **Herbaceous**

If your rock garden has a pond, then this is one of the plants that must go by the waterside. Alternatively, it will do nicely in a damp patch. A rosette of fresh green linear leaves appears in spring and the unusual rose-purple flowers follow in late spring or early summer on stems 30-45cm (12-18in) tall. The 2cm (0.8in) flowers have petals that are twisted and swept back to reveal the protruding yellow anthers.

This is an easy-going plant provided it has some shade and moisture. There are several species, all very similar, which come from damp corners of North America.

Propagation is by division in spring, by removing rooted offsets and potting them in a peaty soil, or by sowing seed in winter so that plants will be ready for setting out in autumn.

Take care
It is essential to label this plant as the leaves die down. 43♦

Dryas octopetala

(Mountain avens)
● **Open situation**
● **Any well-drained soil**
● **Evergreen ground cover**

A native of the European Alps and North America, this plant is a valuable asset to any rock garden, for it pays its rent twice: once with its 4cm (1.6in) wide open creamy white flowers in spring, and secondly with its feathery seedheads in summer. It is a mat-forming plant with small, dark green crinkled oak-like leaves, silver on the reverse, and trailing stems that normally spread to about 60cm (2ft); the plant in our garden is 110 by 110cm (43 by 43in)! The single flowers rise no more than 10cm (4in) above the foliage, with the seedhead slightly taller.

Any soil will do, although the richer it is the less likelihood there is of flowers being produced. Sunshine is also an encouragement to flower. A smaller version, *D. octopetala* 'Minor', is suitable for troughs.

Propagation is from 8cm (3.2in) long heel cuttings, taken in spring or summer and placed around the edge of a pot in sandy soil. Seed is slow to germinate.

Take care
Leave plenty of room to spread. 44♦

Edraianthus pumilio

- **A sunny open position**
- **Well-drained soil**
- **Herbaceous**

This little plant from Dalmatia is related to the campanulas and produces similar flowers. In some catalogues it is still confused with the genus *Wahlenbergia*, which has single flowers. Because of its size and neatness it is eminently suitable for screes or troughs. It forms a small tuft of narrow grey-green leaves from which in summer emerges the cluster of upturned funnel-shaped flowers of lavender blue. The whole plant does not exceed 5-8cm (2-3.2in). It is hardy, although reputed to be short-lived; however, we have had a plant in a trough for five years that has flowered regularly.

Propagation is by sowing seed in winter in a gritty compost, potting on into a limey soil, with limestone chippings incorporated. Water carefully. Soft cuttings of non-flowering wood can be taken in midsummer and inserted in sand, making sure they are stopped from flowering.

Take care
Do not overwater young plants in the winter months. 44♦

Epimedium alpinum

(Barren-wort)
- **Shady corner**
- **Any soil**
- **Semi-evergreen**

A widely distributed genus from the North Temperate regions of Europe and Asia, including Japan. They are particularly useful for ground cover in a semi-woodland or particularly shaded situation. The newly produced leaves in spring are an attractive fresh green, and colour nicely towards the autumn. *E. alpinum*, from the woodlands of Europe, has slightly toothed leaves, turning colour at the edges; it produces attractive racemes of flowers, the outer petals of which are pinky red and the inner bright yellow.

Theoretically the plant is herbaceous, but the old leaves hang on over winter; they should be removed in spring to reveal the flowers before the new leaves grow up to hide them.

Propagation is by division in spring or autumn and potting into a leafy soil. Keep the pots in shade and the young plants will be ready for planting out in four to eight weeks.

Take care
Never let the soil dry out. 45♦

Eranthis hyemalis

(Winter aconite)
- **Prefers semi-shade**
- **Leafy soil**
- **Herbaceous bulb**

A native of Western Europe, this is the species mostly grown in cultivation. Once established it will provide a useful display of bright yellow cupped flowers, 2cm (0.8in) across and 10cm (4in) tall, in late winter and early spring. These flowers are held in a ruff of bright green leaves, which disappear very quickly, leaving no trace of the plants for the rest of the year. This may explain why some people are unable to establish the rhizomes, as they forget where they are planted and disturb them when weeding.

This bulb does better on alkaline soils, but it still appreciates a woodland or semi-shaded site with plenty of leaf-mould incorporated in the soil. It is particularly suited for planting beneath deciduous trees.

Propagation is by seed, sown fresh, either in a seed compost or by allowing self-sown seedlings around the original clump, where they can be lifted and divided later.

Take care
Mark the spot where the tubers are planted and leave undisturbed. 45♦

Erigeron mucronatus

- **Dry sunny position**
- **Enjoys a poor soil**
- **Evergreen**

This is one of those delightful alpine weeds that seed themselves about unobtrusively and do not make a nuisance of themselves. Native to Mexico, it is useful for producing its daisy flowers in summer. It enjoys being starved, among paving or in a stone wall, where the white to deep rose-pink flowers (according to age) provide a dainty show. The whole plant appears delicate, with fragile-looking leaves and wiry stems, but although hit hard by a frost in a bad winter, it will recover. The total height is about 15cm (6in) and the flowers are produced over a long period, well into the autumn.

Propagation is by seed sown in late winter, and the young plants are set out in early summer. It is claimed that no one sows this species more than once, as it seeds itself for ever afterwards!

Take care
Do not be kind or generous to this plant, or it will not give of its best. 46♦

Erinus alpinus
- Sun or shade
- Enjoys growing in crevices
- Evergreen

This is another delightful plant that will provide continuity by seeding itself about, although the individual plants may be short-lived. It is a plant for paving and dry walls, where it will produce a profusion of 7-8cm (2.75-3.2in) wiry stems that bear terminal clusters of small bright pink flowers in summer. There is also a white form, and some named forms with deep crimson or clear pink flowers. It is very desirable and its self-sown seedlings are modest in their behaviour. Seeded into a piece of tufa rock, it makes an attractive show.

Propagation is by seed sown in winter and pricked out into boxes, ready for planting in late spring. Both the species and the colour forms come true from seed, although if they all grow together there may be some variation.

Erysimum 'Jubilee Gold'
- Sunny, open site
- Any well-drained soil
- Short-lived perennial

The dwarf wallflowers provide a colourful display on the rock garden in spring, but regrettably are short-lived. The species keeps itself going by self-sown seedlings, but the named varieties have to be propagated by cuttings. 'Jubilee Gold' forms a low mat of small linear wallflower leaves, which are topped by the golden heads of four-petalled flowers in spring. The parentage of this plant is doubtful, and indeed the whole of this genus and its near relative *Cheiranthus*, with which it has undoubtedly hybridized, is a muddle. Nevertheless these species should not be despised, as there are some good garden plants to be had from them.

Increase by taking cuttings of non-flowering shoots early in the summer and inserting them in the sand frame.

Take care
The more spartan a diet this plant has, the better its performance. 46-7♦

Take care
Do not try to raise 'Jubilee Gold' from seed; it will not come true. 47♦

Erythronium 'Pagoda'

- Requires semi-shade away from sunshine
- Prefers a deep leafy soil
- Bulbous

This is a hybrid between *E. tuolumnense* and one of the species that produces marbled leaves. It is vigorous and free-flowering, with yellow flowers and mottled leaves. The entire genus is extremely hardy and produces worthwhile subjects for the cooler corners of the rock garden in leafy soil. One authority suggests that they like to be in a damp situation beneath trees, which take up excess moisture. They are certainly subjects for the peat and woodland gardens.

E. tuolumnense has been criticized for its small flowers but recently collected forms from its native California have come with 4cm (1.6in) flowers. 'Pagoda', with flower stems 45cm (18in) long, is more robust than its parent *E. tuolumnense*, which can reach a maximum of only 30cm (12in).

Propagation is by fresh seed, sown no later than early autumn.

Take care
Purchase these bulbs from a good dealer, who should pack them in moss or peat to keep moist. 48♦

Euphorbia myrsinites

(Spurge)
- Dry open situation
- Well-drained soil
- Evergreen

This is a plant for a sunny dry spot, where it will retain its compact characteristics. Put in a rich soil it will become straggly and elongated with a tendency for the centre of the plant to get bare-stemmed and unattractive.

It is a slightly succulent plant, exuding a milky liquid if bruised or cut. From a central point it produces a number of yellowish stems that are clothed with blue-grey leaflets; the tips of these stems bear heads of tiny green flowers in conspicuous yellow bracts during early summer. It looks well trailing over the edge of a raised bed.

Propagation is by basal cuttings of non-flowering shoots in late summer, placed in a cutting frame. These should be ready to plant the next spring. Seed sown in late winter is also a means of increase.

Take care
To keep this plant in character, do not feed too generously.

Euryops acraeus

- Sunny situation
- Well-drained soil
- Evergreen shrub

This Basutoland shrub from the Drakensberg Mountains is remarkably hardy in the rock garden. It forms an upright bush, 30cm (12in) high, with bright silver leaves; the pure gold daisy flowers appear on short grey stems in summer.

It was originally thought to be tender, and confined to the alpine house, but it has proved better out of doors by making a neater shaped plant than when under glass. Over the years it forms a compact grey bush when given an open sunny position in a sharply drained soil.

Propagation is by cuttings of non-flowering shoots taken in summer and inserted in a sandy frame. However, there is usually a plentiful supply of suckers around the base of the plant, which can be removed with roots attached and potted up. Although the flowers are attractive, this is a plant grown mainly for its grey foliage.

Take care
Avoid damp situations, and prune the young shrub to a good shape. 48♦

Fritillaria meleagris

(Snake's head fritillary)
- Naturalizes in grass
- Likes a peaty, sandy soil
- Bulbous

A bulb native to Europe, from England to central Russia and south to the southern European Alps and central Yugoslavia, where it can be found in damp meadows. It sends up 30cm (12in) flower stems (with a few linear grey leaves), from which hang one or two wide bells, varying in colour from white with green chequering through to deep chocolate via shades of pinkish lilac and reddish purple. Some named varieties are offered in catalogues.

To succeed in the garden the bulbs must be planted in a situation that never dries out, eg in moist woodland, on the peat garden or by the pond-side. It naturalizes in grass and looks well under shrubs.

Propagation is by seed, bought or collected, which should be sown ripe in late summer immediately after harvesting.

Take care
This plant will thrive only in a damp situation. 65♦

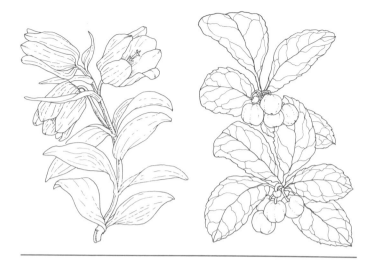

Fritillaria pallidiflora

- Needs moisture when growing
- Well-drained peaty sandy soil
- Bulbous

This whole genus is becoming very popular in gardens and the alpine house, and *F. pallidiflora* from southern Siberia is one of the easiest and most beautiful. The 15-50cm (6-20in) stem bears broadly lanceolate grey leaves, and up to four pendent greenish to luminous yellow 4cm (1.6in) bells appear in the axils of the upper leaves in spring.

It does not require the dampness of the snake's head fritillary, but prefers a good but sharply drained soil in a moderately sunny position, although it will tolerate some shade.

Seed sown in the summer when fresh is a satisfactory method of propagation, and *F. pallidiflora* will flower three years after sowing, which is better than some other species. Bulbils may be found around the parent bulb and these can be detached and grown on.

Take care
Fritillaries should be sown thinly, as the seedlings have to remain *in situ* for a time before transplanting. 66♦

Gaultheria procumbens

(Partridge-berry)
- Partial sunshine
- Leafy lime-free soil
- Evergreen ground cover

This hardy prostrate sub-shrub from North America forms a mat of shiny dark evergreen oval leaves, 2.5cm (1in) long and slightly toothed, which can spread to 1m (39in) or more. Small white or pinkish bell-shaped flowers, about 5-6mm (0.19-0.23in) long, appear at the tips of the shoots in late summer, followed by attractive bright red berries in autumn. The whole plant is no taller than 15cm (6in); it spreads by means of underground stems, and could be termed moderately invasive, although it is easy to control.

G. procumbens is happier in a situation with some but not total sunshine, and appreciates a cool moist leafy soil that is never allowed to dry out.

Propagation is by cuttings taken in early summer and inserted in the peat and sand frame, where they root easily. Pot up into peaty soil during the summer, and over-winter in a frame before planting in spring.

Take care
Allow room to spread. 67♦

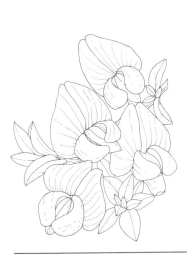
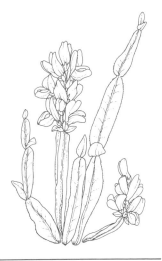

Genista pilosa
- Full sunshine
- Light soil
- Deciduous shrub

Genista sagittalis
- Full sun
- Fairly light soil, good drainage
- Deciduous

There are two forms of this useful free-flowering dwarf shrub from southern Europe: the species itself, which can be as tall as 45cm (18in); and the form 'Prostrata', which is virtually prostrate and will not rise much above 7.5cm (3in). Both produce masses of small yellow pea-like flowers that almost obscure the foliage, and both do well on a sunny bank in the rock garden. *G. pilosa* spreads to about 45cm (18in), but 'Prostrata' will reach 1.2m (4ft) across, contouring over rocks in its path. Any light soil will suit them.

Propagation is not too easy, as seed is not plentiful and cuttings are slow to root. The most proven method is to insert soft cuttings in late spring around the edge of a clay pot, in a mixture of four parts of sand to one of peat. Young plants should not be kept too long in pots as they form a tap-root, which may be damaged when the pot is removed.

This species comes from central and southern Europe. It should appear under its new name, *Chamaespartium sagittale*, but few catalogues will be listing it as such just yet. It is a curious little miniature broom, with branched flowering stems, between 10 and 15cm (4-6in), depending on the richness of the soil. These branched stems have wings, which look like leaves; the actual leaves are small and hairy when young. The small yellow pea-like flowers appear in summer. This plant is good for ground cover, and can spread up to 60cm (2ft).

A much smaller plant, which goes under the name of *Genista delphinensis* in catalogues, is similar in flower and behaviour; this comes from southern France, and is only about 5cm (2in) tall.

Propagation is by taking soft cuttings in summer and inserting them round the edge of a clay pot, in a 4:1 mixture of sand and peat.

Take care
Never plant in a damp situation. 66♦

Take care
This plant prefers a lime-free soil. 67♦

Gentiana acaulis

(Trumpet gentian)
- **Sunny but moist situation**
- **Prefers heavy soils**
- **Evergreen**

Of all the botanical names that are suspect, this is the classic. For years the experts have decreed this to be an invalid name, but everyone continues to use it, and we all know what is meant by *Gentiana acaulis* – the large blue trumpets on the grassy slopes of the Alps.

In gardens, however, they evoke a degree of frustration: either they will flower or they will not, for no apparent reason. They are happiest in a heavy loam and planted firmly. In desperation it has been suggested that they need to be trodden upon deliberately to encourage them to flower, as this emulates the treatment given them by cows in their native habitat. The 5-7.5cm (2-3in) long trumpets appear above mid-green ovate leaves that can form a mat 45cm (18in) across.

Propagation is by division in midsummer, potting into a good loam on the heavy side.

Take care
Move the plant about to encourage flowering. 68♦

Gentiana septemfida

- **Sunny position**
- **Any good garden soil**
- **Herbaceous**

This is the beginner's gentian, and it originates in Asia Minor and Iran. It is easy to grow and flowers well, although it is advisable to choose a plant in flower to be sure of obtaining a good deep blue. It has no particular requirements, growing in most soils without a grumble. The height is 20-30cm (8-12in) and it could spread to 30cm (12in), with the 4cm (1.6in) long flowers appearing in terminal clusters in mid- to late summer. This is a plant that can be relied upon.

Propagation is by seed sown in late summer or midwinter, the only snag being that the seedlings will not be uniform in flower colour. Therefore if you have a good form, take cuttings before it flowers (early summer) and insert them in the sand frame.

Take care
Choose a good form in flower when first purchasing this plant. 69♦

Gentiana sino-ornata

- **Semi-shaded situation**
- **Acid soil**
- **Herbaceous**

Of all the marvellous blue gentians, this is my personal favourite, coming at a time of the year when everything else is disappearing. To see a drift of this plant in autumn is an outstanding memory.

To achieve good results the plants should be divided every two or three years; this is easily done in spring, just as growth is beginning, by separating the thongs and replanting in a lime-free leafy soil. It is well worth the time and effort involved to obtain the best results from this plant, which will reward you with a mass of upturned brilliant blue 5cm (2in) trumpets striped with deeper blue and green-yellow. Several named colour variants are good value, and there is an excellent white form.

Propagation is by division in spring, as mentioned above, planting straight out into leafy soil.

Take care
Divide this plant regularly. 69♦

Gentiana verna

(Spring gentian)
- **Sunny exposure with moisture**
- **Requires a good loam or leaf-mould**
- **Short-lived evergreen**

The form under which this plant is frequently sold is 'Angulosa'. Tufts of light green foliage are formed, from which arise deep blue five-petalled flowers on a 5-7.5cm (2-3in) stem.

This species grows best in a gritty soil rich in humus, and is a lime-lover, though it will tolerate acid soils. Sadly, it tends to be short-lived, but can be replaced by young plants raised from seed. It is a very widespread plant in its native habitats, which are from the west coast of Ireland across to Siberia and Mongolia.

Propagation is best by seed, the plant coming true. Sow fresh seed in late summer and prick out when quite small (four leaves), as larger plants are damaged when moved. Incorporate some limestone chippings in the soil mixture. If fresh seed is not available then sow in late winter, freezing the seed if possible.

Take care
Never transplant mature plants as they have a sensitive root system.

Geranium 'Ballerina'
- Sunny site
- Well-drained soil or scree
- Herbaceous

Geranium dalmaticum
- Open sunny site
- Any light well-drained soil
- Herbaceous

This is reputedly a hybrid of *G. cinereum*, which is a native of rocky habitats in the Pyrenees, southern Italy and parts of the Balkan Peninsula. *G. cinereum* is an easy plant to cultivate in a gritty soil and with some sun. The leaves are deeply cut and grey-green, and make neat mounds about 10cm (4in) high and with a spread of 20-30cm (8-12in). The flowers are a rich crimson-magenta, about 2.5cm (1in) across and on a stem 15cm (6in) tall. They are borne freely from midsummer to autumn. It has a sub-species, *Geranium cinereum* 'Subcaulescens', with larger but paler flowers. However, the hybrid 'Ballerina' is more attractive, with its lilac-pink flowers heavily veined with purple, and slightly greyer leaves.

Propagation is by seed sown in late winter, which will be ready to pot on in early summer for planting the following autumn or spring. Slugs are partial to the young shoots.

Take care
Never give a damp position. 69♦

This is a most attractive and neat plant, which comes – as its name suggests – from Yugoslavia and Albania. It forms a tidy clump, up to 30cm (12in) across, of palmately lobed glossy green leaves, which have a slight tint of red and orange, accentuated in autumn. The sturdy clear pink flowers, 2.5cm (1in) across, are produced on a 20cm (8in) stem over a long period in summer. It is an easy-going plant for full sun and any good soil. There is also a pure white form, 'Album'.

This plant is easily propagated by division: just dig up a portion or the whole plant and literally tear it apart. The resultant offspring will quickly form neat plants, whether put into the garden or nurtured in a pot.

It is such an accommodating plant that little need be given by way of do or do not. Make sure you include this plant in your primary list for the rock garden!

Take care
This species should not be planted in full shade. 70♦

Geum montanum

- Sunny position
- Any good soil
- Evergreen

Although not the most floriferous of plants at any given time, *G. montanum* does produce a succession of rich yellow 2.5cm (1in) wide flowers from mid- to late summer and is thus of value in the rock garden. It is a native of the European Alps, where it forms neat clumps some 20-30cm (8-12in) across and up to 20-25cm (8-10in) tall, with neat crinkly hairy pinnate leaves. It will flower better if grown in a less generous mixture; one authority states that all geums should be starved to give of their best.

A closely related species, *G. reptans,* is occasionally found in cultivation; this differs only in that it has strawberry-like runners from which new plants spring. This latter plant is from two non-limey areas of the European Alps.

Propagation is by division in spring, planting direct into the rock garden.

Take care
If you plant in deep shade, less flowers will be produced.

Gypsophila repens 'Letchworth Rose'

- Sunny open site
- Prefers lime, but tolerates acid soils
- Herbaceous

This is a lime-loving plant, found across Europe from the Juras to the Carpathians and into Spain and central Italy. It forms a flat mat of wiry stems and linear grey-green leaves with a spread of 60-80cm (24-32in). The species may have small white or pink flowers on 7-15cm (2.75-6in) tall stems, which appear throughout the summer. There are several named forms and 'Letchworth Rose' is a good pink.

This is an excellent plant for trailing over rocks, at the edge of a raised bed or on top of a wall, all in sharply drained situations. Although it is lime-loving and does very well in chalky areas, it will grow quite well on acid soils too.

Propagation is by cuttings in early summer, taken before flowering and put in a sand frame; pot on into limey soil, stopping to prevent flowering in the first year. Young plants should be ready in the autumn or the following spring.

Take care
This plant will not do well in shade. 71♦

Haberlea ferdinandi-coburgii
- Shady situation
- Lime-free soil
- Evergreen

Hacquetia epipactis
- Cool position
- Leafy soil
- Herbaceous

This plant is ideal for a shady corner in the rock or peat garden. It is one of a small group of plants that need to be planted on their sides in order to prevent winter damp from nestling in the centre of the rosettes. A rosette of thickish dark green leaves is formed, from which emerges in late spring a 15cm (6in) flower stem bearing up to four tubular pale lilac flowers with crinkled lobes.

This species is ideal for a north-facing peat bed or in a shaded crevice on the rock garden; it prefers soil with plenty of humus.

Propagation is interesting, as this can be done by leaf cuttings. Select material from the centre of the rosette, as the older leaves will not give such a good percentage take. Insert the leaf for one third of its length in a sandy peat mixture in midsummer, making sure that this mixture does not dry out. Young plants should be ready to plant out the following autumn, having over-wintered in a frame.

Take care
Not a plant for sunshine.

It is with a certain amount of hesitation that this plant is included in the list, as it may not be as available as other plants mentioned. It is found locally in woods on the mountains of Eastern Europe and therefore requires a cool position. The peat bed seems to be the ideal place for it, although it will do on a heavier soil. We have a plant in a north-facing peat bed where it does very well.

The plant dies down each summer, and the flowers appear initially as little yellow dots on the soil surface until they emerge to enlarge, ending up by being surrounded by a frill of five green leaves and lasting for quite a while in that state in spring. It does not spread unduly, at most making a clump 20-30cm (8-12in) across.

This species objects to being transplanted, so propagation should be by division in spring, before the plant growth gets going.

Take care
Do not plant in full sun, and remember to label the plant, as it dies down early. 71♦

Above: **Fritillaria meleagris**
A native of damp meadows in the wild, which indicates the requirements of this bulb in gardens. Once planted it should be left undisturbed to seed about. 57♦

Above: **Fritillaria pallidiflora**
Quite a tall fritillary for the rock garden, but it is not obtrusive for long in spring as the foliage dies down quickly. Easy to grow. 58♦

Right: **Gaultheria procumbens**
This mildly vigorous carpet plant has gorgeous berries and good foliage colour in the autumn. 58♦

Below left:
Genista pilosa var. **prostrata**
A useful ground-hugging shrub with miniature broom-like flowers. 59♦

Below right: **Genista sagittalis**
Here the golden-yellow flowers are produced on upright stems. 59♦

Above: **Gentiana acaulis**
The trumpet gentian of the Alps is of the deepest shades of blue, but it is rather temperamental in cultivation, sometimes failing to produce its blue trumpets. Prefers a heavy soil. 60♦

x

Above: **Gentiana septemfida**
One of the easiest of all the gentians to grow, it comes with ease from seed, although variable, and provides a useful display of colour in late summer. 60♦

Right: **Gentiana sino-ornata**
One of the delights of the autumn is to see a bed of these in flower. They prefer a cooler site, with plenty of leaf-mould in the soil. 61♦

Below: **Geranium 'Ballerina'**
This delightful little hybrid produces its pink saucer-shaped flowers lined with maroon stripes in summer, with a few occasional flowers later on. 72♦

Above: **Gypsophila repens
'Letchworth Rose'**
*A frothy mass of pink flowers makes
this a useful plant for tumbling down
a wall or over a rock face.* 63♦

Left: **Geranium dalmaticum**
*Its rosy pink flowers are produced
over a long period in summer, and in
autumn its leaves take on red hues
that extend its period of colour.* 62♦

Right: **Hacquetia epipactis**
*This slightly curious little plant from
Eastern Europe forms its flowers
beneath the ground and then
gradually pushes them above the
surface in early spring.* 64♦

Above left: **Hebe vernicosa**
These shrubby veronicas from New Zealand provide many dwarf shrubs for use in the rock garden. 81♦

Above right:
Helichrysum bellidioides
A carpeting plant with white 'everlasting' papery flowers. 82♦

Left: **Helianthemum 'Ben Dearg'**
There are a number of extremely attractive hybrids in the sun rose family, all very hardy. 82♦

Below: **Houttuynia cordata**
Perhaps on the rather vigorous side, this creeping plant thrives in pondside conditions. 83♦

Above: **Hypericum olympicum 'Citrinum'**
This smaller version of St John's Wort is well-behaved. 84♦

Right:
Iberis sempervirens 'Little Gem'
This neater version of iberis forms a tidy clump. Avoid shady locations. 85♦

Above: **Iris cristata**
*A dwarf iris from the Southern USA
that requires filtered sunlight to give
of its best, so it could be well
accommodated on the peat bed.* 86♦

Right: **Ipheion uniflorum**
*This early-flowering bulb needs to
have its position marked in the
garden, for its foliage dies down early
in the season.* 85♦

Below left: **Iris douglasiana**
*An easy and vigorous plant that will
do well in any soil, either light or
heavy, and is not fussy about
sunshine or shade.* 86♦

Below right: **Iris innominata**
*It is happy, as seen here, in some
sun. It is an extremely variable plant,
preferring a humus-rich soil and
intolerant of lime.* 87♦

Left: **Lamium maculatum 'Beacon Silver'**
Of comparatively recent introduction, this deadnettle is proving to be most useful in filling up odd corners. Very adaptable. 88♦

Right: **Lavandula stoechas**
A native of the warmer climes of the Mediterranean, this lavender has proved to be more hardy than one would expect. Its curiously shaped flowers appear in summer. 89♦

Below: **Leontopodium alpinum**
The edelweiss, a legendary plant of the Alps, is widely supposed to grow in inaccessible crevices, but in fact it is easily found in both scree and grass. Grow in a sunny spot. 90♦

Above: **Lewisia cotyledon**
The lewisias are very popular rock plants from North America. They are almost succulent and so do not like winter wet lying in their rosettes. 90♦

Below: **Linum narbonense**
This fairly tall flax is suitable for the rock garden on account of its dainty behaviour. Its wands of blue flowers wave about in summer. 91♦

Hebe buchananii 'Minor'

- Sunny sheltered position
- Any well-drained soil
- Evergreen shrub

Hebes are basically shrubby veronicas, in which genus they were included at one time. They come from New Zealand and several are suitable for the rock garden – in many cases, more for the foliage than for the flower produced. Some are borderline cases for hardiness, but *H. buchananii* 'Minor' has come through severe winters in our frost pocket of a garden. It forms a bun-shaped cushion, which is created by small dull green leaves set on dense wiry twigs. Reaching no more than 5cm (2in) high, it might make 10-15cm (4-6in) across. The small white stemless flowers appear in midsummer, somewhat sparsely. This is an excellent plant for a sink or trough.

Propagation is in late summer by cuttings inserted in a peat and sand frame. The slow growth will create difficulties in finding cutting material. Cuttings must be kept frost-free the first winter, whilst rooting.

Take care
Although it is basically hardy, do not plant in an exposed situation.

Hebe vernicosa

- Open situation
- Neutral soil
- Evergreen shrub

This attractive hardy shrub comes from New Zealand, where it grows from sea level to 1,500m (4,920ft). Hebes were until recently classified as veronicas, but because of their shrubby nature they have been taken out of that genus. In the main they provide an interesting range of foliage colours, from the grey of *H. pageana* to the golden whipcord stems of *H. armstrongii*.

In severe winters some tend to get cut back, but *H. vernicosa* has proved very hardy. It makes a compact bush, 20cm (8in) tall, with reddish brown stems, and thick fleshy mid-green leaves tipped with pale yellow. The crystalline white flowers, in 2.5cm (1in) wide racemes, appear in midsummer.

Take cuttings of non-flowering shoots with a heel in mid- to late summer; insert in a sand frame and pot up in autumn when rooted, ready to plant out the following spring.

Take care
Make sure this plant is not crowded by its neighbours. 72♦

Helianthemum nummularium 'Ben Dearg'

(Rock rose)
- **Thrives in sunshine**
- **Any well-drained soil**
- **Evergreen**

Rock roses are found throughout Europe except in the north, and produce a wide variety of colours from yellow to deep orange and from pink to deep red. The foliage is grey or green, and the combination of pink flowers and grey foliage, as in the variety 'Wisley Pink', is charming. 'Ben Dearg' flowers are deep copper orange with dark centres.

This group of plants is easy-going and sun-loving, and provides a brilliant display in midsummer. They are, however, rampant, and spread to 60cm (2ft), so care should be taken in siting them; cut back hard after flowering. They seem to thrive well on both acid and alkaline soils.

Propagation is easy: take cuttings of non-flowering shoots, from mid- to late summer, and insert in a peat and sand frame. Pinch out the tips of the plants when they are established in pots.

Take care
Can swamp less vigorous plants. 72♦

Helichrysum bellidioides

- **Sunny exposure**
- **Light, well-drained soil**
- **Evergreen**

The helichrysums come from the Southern Hemisphere and so should be treated as plants of doubtful hardiness. *H. bellidioides* loves to roam around the crevices of rocks and wander through stony ground. It has a degree of aggressiveness in the garden, where it may trample over less uninhibited subjects. It is prostrate, spreading to between 30 and 60cm (1-2ft), with 2cm (0.8in) wide clusters of everlasting flowers appearing in summer. The leaves are an attractive dark green above and woolly-white beneath. It likes a well-drained sunny situation and is hardier than most authorities suggest.

Propagation is by 1.5cm (0.6in) soft cuttings taken in summer and put in a sand frame. These are ready to plant out in autumn or the following spring. Plants can be divided during the summer.

Take care
Make sure it has a warm corner. 73♦

Hepatica transsilvanica

- Shady situation
- Leafy or peaty soil
- Herbaceous bulb

Houttuynia cordata

- Requires very damp situation
- Any soil
- Herbaceous ground cover

This native of Romania is similar to the more widespread and familiarly, but erroneously, named *H. triloba*: the latter should now be *H. nobilis*. *H. transsilvanica* has slightly downy three-lobed leaves, puckered slightly at the edges, and the flowers, which are useful for appearing in very early spring, are mauve-blue, 2.5cm (1in) across, on 10-15cm (4-6in) stems.

This is a plant of the woodlands, and should be given a peaty leaf-mould soil in shaded or semi-shaded conditions. It is ideal for the peat garden. *H. transsilvanica* has been crossed with *H. nobilis* to give *H. × media* 'Ballardii', a superbly robust hybrid.

The plants can be divided in autumn – although this should be confined to large clumps that require moving – and kept in a shaded frame in the winter. Seed should be sown when green.

Take care
Lime should be added to an acid soil.

This species comes from Eastern Asia and is useful for ground cover in damp or waterlogged conditions; it will also thrive under 5cm (2in) of water, so it is useful for the side of a pool. Given the right conditions it can spread rapidly by underground stems and has been described as a 'pretty nuisance'.

Erect 30-45cm (12-18in) stems spring from the ground and have heart-shaped leaves with an almost metallic sheen. At the tip of these appear pure white flowers in midsummer. There is also a double form that is most attractive. The whole plant has a tangy aroma that some find unpleasant.

Propagation is by division in spring or autumn; place pieces of the underground stem, with growing shoots, in a pot of compost and grow on until well rooted.

Take care
Make sure this plant never dries out. 73♦

Hutchinsia alpina

- Partial shade
- Neutral soil
- Evergreen

This is one of the delights on the high mountains of Europe that can be grown with comparative ease in the garden; it is also freely available in the trade, in contrast to some of its endemic companions. It is a tufted perennial up to 5cm (2in) high, with distinctive dark green almost fern-like foliage, and clusters of four-petalled clear white flowers, also 5cm (2in) tall, in early summer.

It requires a cool situation, perhaps in the peat garden, and looks well in a trough, provided it is not in full sun. It would do well in paving, where the roots could keep cool.

Propagation is by seeds sown in midsummer, ie when fresh, and plants will be ready by the following spring. Alternatively it can be divided in spring, planting out direct or potting up.

Take care
Not for a hot, dry, sunny corner.

Hypericum olympicum 'Citrinum'

(St. John's wort)
- Open situation
- Light well-drained soil
- Evergreen

This plant is a member of a large genus of 400 species, not all of which are suitable for the rock garden. Indeed, St. John's wort proper (*H. calycinum*), if planted on the rock garden, would eradicate all competition in about two years.

However, *H. o.* 'Citrinum' is one of the gems from SE Europe, Syria and Asia Minor, and it puts on a good display in summer. Upright slender stems with grey-green leaves form a low mounded bush, and at the end of these 20-25cm (8-10in) stems are borne large (5cm/2in) lemon-yellow flowers with a central boss of similarly coloured stamens. It is said to spread to 60cm (2ft), but in our garden it seeded so much that about 90cm (3ft) was covered.

Unfortunately, seed is variable, so soft cuttings of good forms should be taken in late spring; insert them in a peat and sand frame. Young plants will be ready the following spring.

Take care
Weed out seedlings ruthlessly to keep the plant within bounds. 74►

Iberis sempervirens 'Little Gem'
- **Prefers some sunshine**
- **Any soil**
- **Evergreen**

I. sempervirens is a small evergreen shrub spreading to 45-60cm (18-24in) and it is on the large size for the smaller rock garden; but in the larger rock garden its 4cm (1.6in) wide flowerheads make a splash of white in early summer. It comes from the mountains of southern Europe, around the Mediterranean.

For the average or small rock garden the form 'Little Gem' is recommended, because this spreads only to about 25cm (10in) and is 10cm (4in) tall. Its flowerhead is slightly smaller and it has attractive tight greeny buds.

Propagation is by short – up to 5cm (2in) – softwood cuttings taken from non-flowering shoots between mid- and late summer and inserted in the peat and sand frame. Over-winter the rooted cuttings in potting compost in a cold frame.

Flea beetles, common to the cabbage family, may eat small holes in the leaves. Dust with derris.

Take care
Avoid total shade. 75♦

Ipheion uniflorum
- **Sunny well-drained site**
- **Any soil**
- **Herbaceous bulb**

This poor plant has suffered from several name changes, and may still be listed as *Milla, Tritelia, Brodiaea* or *Tristagma*. It is a free-flowering bulb, producing several 15cm (6in) flower stems on which are held funnel-shaped six-pointed star-shaped flowers, from white to deep blue in colour; some colour forms have been given varietal names.

This plant, endemic to South America, is an attractive species for the garden, where all it needs is a sunny well-drained spot where it can remain undisturbed. The bulbs and pale leaves are said to have an onion smell, but I must confess to never having noticed. Mark the spot where this species is planted, as the leaves die down soon after flowering.

Propagation is by digging up the clumps and separating the young bulbs. These should be planted straight away and not allowed to become dry. This division is best done immediately after flowering.

Take care
Does not like to be disturbed. 77♦

Iris cristata
- **Likes semi-shade**
- **Grows in a neutral soil**
- **Herbaceous**

It is extremely difficult to suggest a representative cross-section of this genus, which offers so much to rock gardens. The most easily obtained *I. reticulata* forms are so well known as not to need space here. The yellow *I. danfordiae* is also an excellent early spring bulb.

I. cristata has been described as one of the best of all the dwarf irises. The rhizome produces a fan of leaves up to 15cm (6in) long, from which arise one or two flowers about 3-4cm (1.25-1.6in) in diameter; these vary from lilac to purple or violet, but the form in general circulation is lilac-blue. It is a native of moist woods in eastern North America, and therefore prefers peat soil and good drainage.

Propagation forms part of the cultivation routine for this plant, which should be lifted, divided and replanted from time to time, because it tends to die in the centre. Do this after flowering.

Take care
Never put this plant on a dry site. 76♦

Iris douglasiana
- **Tolerates sunshine or shade**
- **Accepts any soil condition**
- **Evergreen**

This is a very tough and free-flowering iris from the Pacific coast of North America; unfortunately, it is also very variable. It is 15-70cm (6-28in) tall and the broad leaves are up to 2cm (0.8in) wide. The branched flower stems have flowers 7-10cm (2.75-4in) in diameter, which vary from lavender to purple, with darker veins and a yellowish spot on the falls (outer petals); these appear in early summer.

This plant benefits from a cool site in the rock garden, as its native habitat is in fields and light woodland.

Propagate with seed saved from the best forms, and sow in the autumn or spring in a temperature of 7-10°C (45-50°F) in a seed compost. Plant the seedlings in spring when they are quite small, as the rhizomes resent disturbance when more mature; they will flower the following year. To maintain a good form, detach a young rhizome in the autumn and replant.

Take care
Never let young plants dry out. 76♦

Iris innominata

- Likes full sunshine
- Requires a good lime-free soil
- Herbaceous

This American species, from Oregon this time, is also variable, but has most attractively proportioned flowers in several shades, ranging from blue to mauve and from yellow to bronze, at midsummer. The 6.5-7.5cm (2.6-3in) flowers are carried singly on a stem 15-25cm (6-10in) tall, with many narrow leaves of the same height.

This species detests lime in the soil, and is therefore a subject for the open peat bed or rock garden with humus-rich soil. Experiences vary with this plant, but if soil conditions and moisture are correct, then it can take full sun.

I. innominata has been crossed with *I. douglasiana* to produce the 'Californian Hybrids'. Select good forms only for increasing by division; otherwise propagation is as for *I. douglasiana*.

Iris reticulata

- Full sun or partial shade
- Any well-drained soil
- Herbaceous bulb

The late winter-flowering irises are one of the delights of the garden, poking their way through the ground at an inhospitable time of year. Their native habitat is near the snowline at 3000m (9,843ft) in central Turkey, the Caucasus and Iran, which shows their hardiness.

The flowers vary in colour from light blue to deep violet and some of these colour forms have been given cultivar names: 'Harmony' is deep blue; 'Cantab' is a good light blue; 'J.S.Dijt' is a distinctive deep red-purple. There are many others and catalogues should be consulted. The flowers are about 6-8cm (2.4-3.2in) wide and 15cm (6in) tall, with narrow squarish leaves eventually rising well above the dying flowers. Bulbs should be planted in autumn. They thrive on a light, well-drained soil and are tolerant of lime.

Propagate by division of the bulbs in midsummer or by seed, but the latter gives variable results.

Take care
This plant detests lime.77◗

Take care
For best results this plant likes some chalk or lime in the soil.

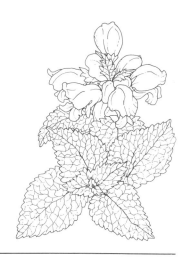

Juniperus communis 'Compressa'

- Any situation
- Any well-drained soil
- Evergreen conifer

For reasons of space, only one conifer can be included in this list of alpines. To have to choose one out of the dozens available was not too difficult, as *J. communis* 'Compressa' is one of the neatest of them all, forming an upright column, eventually reaching 60cm (2ft), but probably taking up to 15 years to attain that height. They are very effective when planted in clumps, if there is room, and they do very well in troughs. On the rock garden, plant them at the base of a rock; they tend to look unnatural on top, where they stick up like a sore thumb.

Propagate by removing young green shoots in midsummer from parts of the plant that will not spoil its looks; these shoots should have some mature wood at their base. Insert them in a sand frame, where they may have to over-winter before potting up.

Take care
Do not plant in a wet or damp spot.

Lamium maculatum 'Beacon Silver'

- Sunny or shady situation
- Any soil
- Ground cover

This is a plant of very recent introduction, which could be considered a degree too coarse for the more orderly rock garden. However, it has most attractive silver foliage, edged with green, with interesting – but not important – blue-mauve dead-nettle flowers. It thrives on well-drained acid soil, and makes a carpet some 1.5m (5ft) across. In late summer the leaves have small blotches of colour to match the flowers.

This is obviously a plant to be put in a carefully chosen site, where its invasive tendencies can be either curbed or given full rein. It is happy in either sun or shade, but gives a better foliage colour in full sun. A starvation diet would curb this plant's zest for life, but it would still require moisture.

Propagation is by division in spring when growth is just starting; pull the clump apart and replant.

Take care
Never plant near anything of value and watch out for slugs, as it is a favourite meal for them. 78♦

Lavandula stoechas
(French lavender)
- **Well-drained open situation**
- **Warm, light soil**
- **Almost hardy shrublet**

Common lavender is far too large for any rock garden, but its miniature cousin from the Mediterranean region – which forms a small bush up to 30cm (12in) tall in gardens, although taller in the wild – is a most suitable subject. Its slightly curious four-angled spikes of deep purple flowers, topped by a tuft of ovate purple bracts that persist after the plant has faded, appear in summer. It has the normal grey-green leaves of lavender.

Coming from the Mediterranean area, it does possess a degree of tenderness, but this can be overcome by keeping a supply of young plants. Either sow seed in February in a seed compost, or take cuttings of non-flowering shoots in early autumn and over-winter them in a frame.

Leiophyllum buxifolium
- **Semi-shade**
- **Moist peaty soil**
- **Dwarf shrub**

A native of eastern North America, this small shrub is ideal for the peat garden, where it will thrive in the moister conditions. Moisture is a particular requirement when the plant is young and it appreciates some light, but not full sun. It forms an evergreen bush some 30cm (12in) high; its small round leathery leaves are glossy green, and the starry five-petalled flowers are produced in terminal clusters, 2.5cm (1in) across, in early summer. However, it is at its most attractive when the flowers are unopened, at the pink bud stage. There is a smaller form, 'Prostratum', which is only 7.5-15cm (3-6in) tall.

Propagate by cuttings taken with a heel in mid- to late summer and inserted in a peaty compost in a shaded frame. Pot on, pinch out and keep in a frame for their first winter.

Take care
Make sure this plant has a sunny corner to itself. 79♦

Take care
This is not a plant for a hot sunny aspect, nor does it like chalk or lime.

Leontopodium alpinum

(Edelweiss)
- Well-drained situation
- Light soil
- Herbaceous

To many, the beginning and end of alpines is the edelweiss: stories are told of the apparently impossible locations on steep cliffs in which this species grows, but in fact it is a rather dreary plant that is easily found in meadows at no great height in the Alps.

A clump of narrow grey basal leaves is formed, which puts forth a 15cm (6in) flower stem at the top of which is borne a flat head of what can best be described as rayless daisies. The whole plant is covered with white woolly hairs. It is undoubtedly a curious plant that provides a talking point, and it grows very happily in any well-drained sunny situation.

Propagation is by seed sown in winter, ready for pricking out in spring and planting in autumn.

Take care
Put near a more colourful plant, either to tone down the other colour or to enhance the dullness of the edelweiss! 78-79♦

Lewisia cotyledon

- Requires moisture in summer
- Prefers acid soil
- Evergreen

This valuable genus of plants from North America produces many showy plants that are essential for the rock garden. When plants hybridize, they sometimes produce inferior seedlings, but not so the lewisias, which produce some wonderful colour forms in the pink, peach and apricot to orange range. The plant forms a thick caudex (root stock), which produces almost succulent fleshy leaves, and 15-30cm (6-12in) tall flower spikes of many blooms in early summer.

This plant thrives on a rich diet, but in well-drained gritty soil. It prefers to be planted on its side in the garden and only just tolerates chalk, preferring more acid conditions. *L. cotyledon* and its many colour forms and variations are excellent for the alpine house, where they enjoy a drying-off period after flowering.

Propagation is by seed.

Take care
Plant on its side in a rock crevice to prevent winter wetness rotting the rosette of leaves. 80♦

Linnaea borealis
(Twin-flower)
- **Shady position**
- **Leafy or peaty soil**
- **Ground cover**

The generic name of this plant commemorates the celebrated Carl von Linné (Linnaeus), the Swedish botanist. It is a plant that can be found in the colder regions of the Northern Hemisphere, which testifies to its hardiness. Forming a mat, it sends its wiry stems hither and thither in a tangle, from which emerge several delicate pink bell-shaped flowers in pairs on 5cm (2in) stems.

In ideal conditions, such as a cool aspect in shade or a north-facing peat bed, *L. borealis* will make a mat up to 60cm (2ft) wide. There is also a slightly larger American form.

Propagation is tricky: it is necessary to grow a young plant on fast in a pan of sandy leaf-mould, which should be kept well watered from spring to autumn, and less so in winter. The runners should be pinned down to encourage rooting and then removed the following spring, ready for potting up and planting out in the autumn.

Take care
This is not a plant for full sunshine.

Linum narbonense
(Flax)
- **Sunny position**
- **Light soil**
- **Herbaceous**

This is a rather tall plant for the smaller rock garden, but its elegant 50cm (20in) arching stems are thin enough to be accommodated unobtrusively and without looking too gross. It is a native of southern Europe, but is hardy in all but the severest winters and not fussy over soil or situation. The addition of peat or leaf-mould seems to help, although in the wild it is native to calcareous soils.

The 2.5cm (1in) wide rich blue flowers appear at the tips of the graceful stems in summer and provide a succession of colour. It usually dies back in winter, but in favoured localities it may persist as an evergreen.

Propagation is by seed sown in winter, ready for potting up in spring and planting out in mid- to late summer. If you have a good form, try soft basal cuttings in spring or take firmer cuttings late in the summer.

Take care
Plant this in the sunshine. 80◗

Lithodora diffusa 'Grace Ward'

- Well-drained open site
- Acid soil
- Evergreen

This plant has undergone a name change, and may still be found in catalogues as *Lithospermum diffusum*. The type species is rarely seen nowadays, being replaced by named clones of which 'Grace Ward' now seems to have superseded 'Heavenly Blue'. A 60cm (2ft) wide mat of rough dark green foliage is formed, which is covered with deep blue flowers in early summer.

Its requirements are particular if it is going to look its best, for it hates lime and prefers a sandy soil with plenty of peat and leaf-mould incorporated, in full sun.

Successful propagation is very precise. In the Northern Hemisphere take soft green cuttings after the first week in July and before the second week in August. (In the Southern Hemisphere this would be January and February respectively.) The percentage of germination is much higher during this period. Water before and after taking cuttings.

Take care
This plant needs moisture. 97♦

Lithophragma parviflora

- Appreciates woodland conditions
- Leafy acid soil
- Herbaceous

Although – as its name suggests – the flowers are small, they make up for that disadvantage by producing sufficient on a flowering stem to make a show. It is one of those plants that either will take to your garden (giving you cause to complain that it is invasive) or will be slow to establish (making those who cannot grow it envious). It is a delightful woodlander from North America and thrives in peaty soil and light shade. The root consists of grain-like bulblets and these produce orbicular basal leaves, which are cut into three sections that in themselves are three-lobed, so they end up looking much divided. The 15cm (6in) flower stems have heads of deeply fringed pale pink flowers. It is an attractive plant for the peat garden in partial shade.

Propagation is by division in early spring, when growth is being started; the bulblets transplant well at this stage.

Take care
Do not plant in alkaline conditions. 97♦

Lychnis alpina
- Full sun
- Moist lime-free soil
- Evergreen

Lysimachia nummularia 'Aurea'
- Sun or semi-shade
- Any soil
- Herbaceous ground cover

This plant has suffered from a name turnabout, returning now to its original name. It forms a tuft of dark green linear leaves, from which arise 10-15cm (4-6in) flowering stems with a cluster of bright rose flowers that appear from late spring to midsummer. It is happiest in a lime-free soil that can be kept moist. It is not a typical peat bed plant, as it requires full sun, but it does well there. It is widespread from Northern Europe across to Siberia and Labrador.

Propagation is by seed sown in late winter in a peat-based seed compost. Prick out after one month and pot on for planting in late spring. Supplies of this plant should be kept going, as it has a reputation for being short-lived.

Although this is a vigorous trailing plant it is not beyond control and therefore has a place on the rock garden for both its foliage and its flowers. It is also good for bulb cover. The type species is a native of Europe, including Great Britain, and is found growing by the waterside, but it has adapted to growing in drier conditions in gardens. Although technically evergreen, its foliage can hardly be considered very attractive in winter. The yellow upright-facing cup-shaped flowers match the yellow foliage and appear in midsummer.

Propagate by division and replanting in midsummer, taking care to keep the divisions moist.

Take care
Do not plant on a dry chalky soil.

Take care
Although adapted to dry conditions, this plant grows best in a moist spot.

Mimulus luteus guttatus

(Monkey musk)
- **Likes moisture**
- **Any soil**
- **Herbaceous**

This genus needs careful placing on the rock garden because of its flamboyant colours. However, the requirements of the plant virtually dictate its habitat, for it needs a fair bit of moisture. By the side of a pond or stream would be ideal, otherwise a cool moist spot on the rock garden. *M. luteus* itself is rather tall for the rock garden, as it can reach 60cm (2ft); so it is to its sub-species *guttatus* that we turn, with its 4cm (1.6in) wide yellow flowers, blotched with brown-purple, on 15-20cm (6-8in) stems. Its leaves are a fresh green; the stems have a tendency to flop, although basically it is not an untidy plant. It may be found listed in some catalogues as *M. langsdorfii*.

Propagation is either by seed in winter, sown under glass and kept at 13-16°C (55-60°F); or more readily by cuttings or division in spring, when new plants are ready within two or three weeks.

Take care
Not a plant for a hot sunny corner. 98♦

Narcissus bulbocodium

(Hoop petticoat daffodil)
- **Moist situation**
- **Grows well in grass**
- **Bulbous**

It is surprising that this bulb, which comes from SW France, Spain, Portugal and NW Africa, is so hardy in gardens. Flowering in late winter or early spring, it comes at a thin time of year for flowers. It is excellent value and – given the right conditions – will naturalize in grass. There are many varieties.

The funnel-shaped corona, which gives rise to its common name because of its resemblance to a crinoline, dominates the petals entirely. These 2-5cm (0.8-2in) long trumpets appear on stems up to 15cm (6in) tall. As mentioned, this bulb does well in grass, and will tolerate a peat bank if it is not too shady or too dry.

Propagation is by division every three or four years, digging up and separating the clumps of bulbs. Otherwise the seed can be used, and in many cases it sows itself naturally.

Take care
In turf, mark where the bulbs are and cut the grass in late summer. 99♦

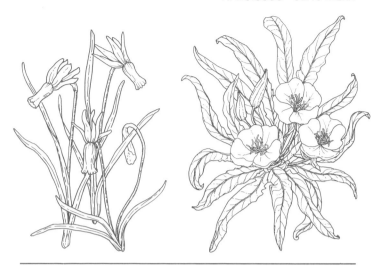

Narcissus cyclamineus
- **Damp situation**
- **Leafy soil**
- **Bulbous**

Flowering 10-14 days earlier than *N. bulbocodium*, this is another bulb for naturalizing, perhaps in damper conditions. It has a curious and distinctive appearance in that the petals are swept back from the narrow tube-like corona. This reflexed habit is persistent in the numerous hybrids from this species. The height of the flower stems is never less than 10cm (4in), and taller in shade; the total length of the flower itself is 3.5-4cm (1.3-1.6in) and the colour is a bright rich yellow.

This species is happy in quite damp conditions where it will seed happily along the banks of streams and in woodlands.

Propagation is by seed, sown at midsummer when ripe in the open ground or in a pot, where it should not be allowed to dry out. They should be left *in situ* for at least two years, until the small bulbs have formed. They begin to flower in the third or fourth year after sowing.

Take care
Does not appreciate a hot dry site. 98♦

Oenothera missouriensis
- **Sunny site**
- **Any soil**
- **Herbaceous**

As its name suggests, this is a plant from the south central USA; it may be found catalogued in some countries as *Megapterium missouriense*. It is valuable for its long flowering period in the summer months, when it provides a succession of 6-8cm (2.4-3.2in) wide lemon-yellow almost stemless flowers. The whole plant is no taller than 10-15cm (4-6in) because of the floppy habit of the flowering stems, which lie prostrate on the ground.

Although demanding of space – for it can spread up to 60cm (2ft) – it is not otherwise demanding in its requirements. A normal soil in a sunny position will encourage its flowers to open in the evenings, and they will last for several days.

Propagation is by seed in winter, potting up in spring and planting out in late spring or early summer. Cuttings can be taken in late summer to over-winter in a frame, and these will be ready to plant in the spring.

Take care
Label plant; it fades in winter. 99♦

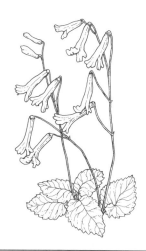

Omphalodes verna

- Semi-shade
- Peaty or leafy soil
- Herbaceous

This plant is one for the shaded end of the rock garden or woodland conditions elsewhere, because it enjoys a leafy soil. It comes from the European Alps and is one of the earliest of its genus to flower; the 1cm (0.4in) wide bright blue blooms are freely produced in terminal clusters during late winter and continue into the spring. There is also a white form that is not unattractive. The plant is very well-behaved, spreading not more than 30cm (12in), and is about 15cm (6in) tall. It spreads by means of runners, but it is not invasive. It does very well on a poor soil.

Propagate by division in spring or autumn, planting out direct or potting on in a John Innes No. 2 potting compost.

Take care
Do not confuse this with *O. luciliae*, which requires full sun and open drainage.

Ourisia coccinea

- Cool shaded position
- Lime-free soil
- Evergreen

This is a plant with confused nomenclature: the plant originally called *O. coccinea* is now known as *O. elegans*. The plant described here is what is known today as *O. coccinea*. The ourisias come from the Southern Hemisphere and this one is from the Chilean Andes. Thus they can be considered hardy, although in practice they have somewhat precise requirements in the garden: moist in summer and dry in winter, the reverse of most gardens. It prefers well-drained leafy, peaty soil in a shady situation: against a north wall would be perfect. It does run about a bit, but it produces its welcome scarlet trumpets, which are carried loosely on 20cm (8in) stems and arise from a mat of ovate leaves. This mat can spread up to 45cm (18in) if it likes you.

Propagate by division in spring, potting in peaty soil and keeping the young plants in a shady place for four to six weeks, until they are ready for planting.

Take care
Not a plant for full sun and dry soil.

Above:
Lithodora diffusa 'Grace Ward'
Formerly Lithospermum, *this plant produces its deep blue flowers over a wide mat of rough leaves.* 92♦

Below: **Lithophragma parviflora**
This attractive plant with pale pink flowers likes a cool situation where its grain-like bulblets can spread about and increase. 92♦

Above: **Narcissus bulbocodium**
The hoop petticoat daffodil is a very accommodating dwarf bulb for early spring, when its yellow flowers are produced in profusion. 94♦

Above left: **Mimulus guttatus**
The musks generally prefer a damp situation where they are at their happiest, spreading and producing their yellow flowers in profusion. 94♦

Left: **Narcissus cyclamineus**
This unusual-looking dwarf daffodil with its swept-back petals will naturalize along a damp ditch and flower well. 95♦

Below: **Oenothera missouriensis**
The dwarf evening primroses make a good showing with their freely produced yellow trumpet-shaped flowers. Although the flowers die quickly, they keep coming. 95♦

Above: **Penstemon newberryi**
*There are numerous penstemons
from North-west America ranging
from pink through to blue. This one
forms a shrub that spreads about to
produce its pink flowers.* 114♦

Left: **Oxalis adenophylla**
*Some oxalis are straightforward
weeds and should be avoided, but
O.adenophylla is bulbous and well-
behaved and enjoys being planted in
full sunshine.* 113♦

Right: **Parahebe catarractae**
*A shrubby plant from New Zealand
that is happy tumbling through rocks;
it flowers well, given a sunny well-
drained situation.* 113♦

Above: **Pimelea coarctata**
This is another delightful New Zealand miniature shrub, with small grey leaves, and scented white flowers in early summer. 115♦

Left: **Polygala chamaebuxus 'Rhodoptera'**
This colourful subject is a small shrubby plant that will thrive in the peat garden. 116♦

Bottom left:
Phlox 'Chattahoochee'
This is a quite outstanding plant for the cooler part of the rock garden or peat bed, where it will form a loose spreading clump 114♦

Below: **Phlox 'Daniel's Cushion'**
This is one of the P.subulata cultivars that is less spreading than its close relatives. Flowers in late spring. 115♦

Above: **Polygonum affine 'Darjeeling Red'**
This autumn-flowering knotweed *produces its upright spikes at a useful time of year. The flowers open up to pink from the red buds.* 117♦

Above: **Potentilla crantzii**
A sun-loving and summer-flowering plant from Arctic areas of Europe, Asia and America; its yellow flowers have a basal orange blotch. 118♦

Below: **Polygonum vaccinifolium**
Another of the knotweeds, but with smaller flowers that last almost to midwinter. It is at its best cascading down a wall. 117♦

Above: **Primula denticulata**
The drumstick primula is one of the easiest grown alpines, and a good plant for the beginner. 118♦

Left: **Primula juliae**
A spreading miniature pink primrose, good for edges of borders. 119♦

Above right: **Primula vialii**
A further variation on the primula theme, this time from China. 120♦

Right: **Ptilotrichium spinosum**
This grey-leaved shrublet also has a pink-flowered form 121♦

Left: **Ramonda myconi**
This is an alpine that prefers not to have winter wet standing in its rosette, so it is happier when planted on its side, where it will produce its blue flowers freely. 122♦

Right: **Ranunculus gramineus**
This buttercup with grass-like leaves produces its cup-shaped flowers on tallish stems in late spring. 123♦

Below:
Ranunculus ficaria 'Flore Plena'
The double form of the lesser celandine enjoys the damp conditions of a wet ditch, where it flowers prolifically in spring. Do not allow the plant to dry out. 122♦

Above: **Rhododendron 'Blue Tit'**
One of the dwarf rhododendrons that are invaluable on the rock garden or peat bank. Remember that they do not like alkaline soils 124♦

Right: **Rhodohypoxis baurii 'Margaret Rose'**
One of the several cultivars of these hardy bulbs from South Africa, which do surprisingly well outdoors north of the Equator. 124♦

Below: **Roscoea cautleoides**
This less common plant has unusual flowers that thrive in the moist cool conditions of the peat bed. It is a summer-flowering plant that requires light shade. 125♦

Above **Salix arbuscula**
The dwarf willows provide some interesting shapes and textures for the rock garden, though some of them are rather vigorous. 126♦

Below: **Sagina procumbens 'Aurea'**
This mat-forming pearlwort has an attractive yellow foliage that is useful for contrast in an alpine lawn. 125♦

Oxalis adenophylla

- Sunny, well-drained site
- Any soil
- Herbaceous

Some members of the oxalis genus are extremely invasive – so much so, that the New Zealand Department of Agriculture has banned the importation of certain species. However, others possess more refined ways of behaviour and one such is *O. adenophylla* from Chile. It has a fibre-coated bulbous rhizome from which arise 2cm (0.8in) wide greyish leaves. The 4cm (1.6in) wide light magenta to near white solitary flowers with a satiny sheen appear in early summer.

This species is perfectly hardy, but thrives in a sunny position with good drainage. It dies down in winter.

Propagation is by removing the off-set side bulbs in early spring, either planting them out or potting up in gritty soil.

This is a charming genus, with two other South American species that should be tried in the alpine house: *O. enneaphylla* in its delightful pink form 'Rosea', and *O. laciniata* with deep mauve, almost blue, flowers.

Take care
Label this plant, as its foliage dies down early in the season. 100♦

Parahebe catarractae

- Well-drained site in scree
- Neutral soil
- Evergreen

Related to the veronicas and hebes, where it may sometimes be found listed, this sub-shrub is of garden origin. Care should be taken to obtain the correct plant; one listed as *Hebe catarractae* is totally different in height and colour.

P. catarractae, its name giving an idea of its behaviour, requires a neutral soil and a little sun; it looks its best when it can tumble down between rocks. It bears ovate mid-green leaves and produces in summer a mass of terminal sprays of loosely borne white flowers, with a purple central zone, giving rise to some descriptions of 'purple-white'.

Propagation is by soft cuttings taken from mid- to late summer and inserted in a sandy frame. Make sure to stop them to produce neat plants, which will be ready by the next spring.

Take care
Propagate this plant for continuity of stock. 101♦

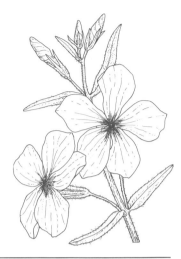

Penstemon newberryi

- ● Warm, well-drained site
- ● Any soil
- ● Semi-evergreen

This plant is sometimes confused with *P. menziesii*, which it resembles. This is another genus where there is considerable confusion of names. There are a number of attractive species, whatever their correct names may be, mostly originating in North America. Though technically hardy, they do suffer in severe winters, so a stock of young plants should be kept in reserve. They do well in any open, well-drained soil, but an excess of moisture may kill them.

P. newberryi will form a bushy sub-shrub some 20cm (8in) tall and will spread to 30-40cm (12-16in). Racemes of snapdragon-like pink to rose-purple flowers, about 3-4cm (1.25-1.6in) long, appear in midsummer.

Propagation is by 5-7.5cm (2-3in) long cuttings, taken in late summer or early autumn, which will be ready by the next spring. Seed, sown in winter, is very variable.

Take care
Avoid wet conditions. 100-101♦

Phlox 'Chattahoochee'

- ● Light shade
- ● Peaty soil
- ● Herbaceous

This invaluable genus, native to North America, includes species that like a variety of conditions. 'Chattahoochee' is a variety happiest in cool peaty conditions. It is rather sprawling, but makes up for that possible disadvantage by producing 15-20cm (6-8in) tall heads of deep lavender 3cm (1.25in) wide flowers, each with a crimson eye.

The flower season extends from spring onwards, which is good for colour but makes difficulties in propagation, as each shoot bears flowering heads and there is rarely non-flowering material suitable for cuttings. Where possible, cuttings should be taken and placed in the sand and peat frame. Plants that are raised from seed vary considerably, and mostly have the crimson eye missing; however, they will all have the same prolonged flowering period, unlike either of the putative parents: *P. pilosa* and *P. divaricata*.

Take care
Do not put this plant in full sun. 102♦

 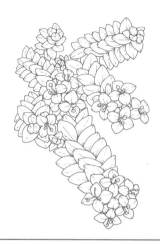

Phlox subulata 'Daniel's Cushion'
- Open sunny situation
- Neutral soil
- Evergreen

The true species of this technically sub-shrubby plant is never seen in cultivation, having been supplanted by several named varieties, lists of which can be found in specialist catalogues. 'Apple Blossom' is pale pink; 'G. F. Wilson', clear lilac; and 'Temiscaming', a brilliant magenta-red. These form spreading mats up to 45cm (18in) across and no more than 10cm (4in) tall when in flower; they look particularly well cascading over rocks and dry walls, producing their 1.5-2cm (0.6-0.8in) wide flowers *en masse* in late spring.

'Daniel's Cushion', however, has a less spreading tendency, possibly a maximum of 25-30cm (10-12in) at most, and so is suitable for the scree or where it cannot be over-shadowed by taller plants.

Propagation is by soft cuttings taken in mid- to late summer and inserted in a sand frame.

Take care
Do not put more vigorous subjects near this variety. 103♦

Pimelea coarctata
- Sunny sheltered position
- Lime-free soil
- Evergreen shrub

This is another plant that has name problems. It may also be listed as *P. prostrata*, of which it is also said to be a congested form. The plant under description forms flat mats of leafy twigs; the leaves are grey-green and tiny, occasionally rimmed red. The flowerheads are borne at the tips of the many twigs: although the individual waxy white flowers are minute, there are so many that they form a mass. The plant rises only a few centimetres off the ground, but a happy plant will spread to 60cm (24in). After it flowers in early summer, fleshy white berries appear.

It likes a moist but well-drained soil, and where it is happy the stems will root as they spread. This gives a direct clue to propagation, as these rooted twigs can be removed and potted up in autumn for spring planting.

Take care
This plant needs protection from extreme cold. 103♦

Pleione formosana

- Shady situation
- Good humus-rich soil
- Herbaceous pseudobulb

It can be said that this is one of the aristocrats of the rock garden, producing its hardy flowers in spring. It may be offered more correctly as *P. bulbocoides,* as the naming of this genus is still confused. This orchid species certainly looks well, even exotic, when grown in a protected corner of the peat garden, where it can be kept on the dry side during its dormant stage in winter. To this end a protective pane of glass will be useful.

It must be said that most growers tend to keep this plant indoors in pots, but as they produce plenty of spare pseudobulbs it is worth planting some out. The mature green pseudobulbs are about 2.5cm (1in) tall with 7.5cm (3in) wide pink and white orchid-like flowers produced on stems up to 15cm (6in) long. The ribbed leaves are slightly longer.

Propagate by removing the young pseudobulbs and planting in a sandy compost.

Take care
Never plant in full sunshine.

Polygala chamaebuxus

(Ground box)
- Light shade
- Peaty, leafy soil
- Evergreen sub-shrub

This plant from the Alps does well in gardens. It forms small bushes 10-15cm (4-6in) tall with box-like leaves and a spread of about 20-30cm (8-12in). Cream and yellow flowers tipped with purple appear from late spring to midsummer, up to six flowers on each stem. In the form illustrated, the flowers are carmine and yellow, and thus slightly more spectacular. This may be seen catalogued as 'Purpurea', 'Rhodoptera' or 'Grandiflora'.

Growing as it does on the edge of woodland, this species appreciates a leafy soil and some light shade.

Propagation is by soft cuttings taken in mid- to late summer and inserted in the shaded peat frame. Pot on, making sure to pinch out the tips to obtain a bushy plant. The plants can be divided in spring.

Take care
Not a plant for a hot sunny corner. 102▶

Polygonum affine 'Darjeeling Red'

- **Any situation**
- **Any soil**
- **Ground cover**

Although this species is vigorous, and covers an area up to 45cm (18in) across, it is invaluable for its upright spikes of clear pink flowers in late summer and early autumn. 'Darjeeling Red' is as vigorous, but the 15cm (6in) flower spikes are deep pink. The narrow dark green leaves turn bronzy red in winter, finishing up as an acceptable russet-brown in midwinter.

Any soil or situation will suit this species, but perhaps full shade and damp would not encourage it to produce so many flowers. This is an accommodating and completely hardy plant.

Propagation is by division in early spring as growth begins; plant out direct or pot up in a normal compost.

Polygonum vaccinifolium

- **Sunny situation**
- **Any soil**
- **Ground cover**

The spikes of this vigorous plant extend the flowering season well into the autumn and it is sometimes possible to pick a small bunch of its pink spikes on Christmas Day. Although it will cover the ground, it looks best cascading down a dry wall or over a rock face. The small pointed oval leaves take on autumn tints, and the slender rose-pink flower spikes rise 5-10cm (2-4in) from the flat mat.

P. vaccinifolium will give of its best in a light well-drained soil and sunny position, although it is quite hardy. Despite its vigorous habits it is by no means invasive, and can easily be kept under control.

Propagation is by division in spring or autumn, or by cuttings taken from midsummer onwards and inserted in the sand frame.

Take care
Do not give too rich a diet, or it may produce soft leafy growth instead of flowers. 105♦

Take care
May swamp less vigorous plants. 104♦

Potentilla crantzii

- **Sunny exposure**
- **Any soil**
- **Herbaceous**

An inhabitant of grassy meadows in the Alps, North America and Asia, this species is both useful and hardy. It forms a tuft of 5-15cm (2-6in) stalks, with small palmate leaves and broad-petalled yellow flowers blotched orange at the base of each petal.

The flowering period in gardens is mid- to late summer, and the length of the flowering stem depends on the plant's environment and whether it is drawn up by its neighbours. It does well on a light open soil and in full sun, where it will flower well. In its native habitat it lives in a limey soil, but in cultivation it is quite accommodating in this respect.

There are two ways of propagating this plant: by seed, in late winter or early spring, though this may not result in the right plant; and by division in the autumn, which is preferable.

Take care
Do not let this plant be over-shadowed. 105♦

Primula denticulata

(Drumstick primula)
- **Any situation**
- **Any soil**
- **Herbaceous**

One of the easiest, most reliable and most accommodating plants for the rock garden. Its globose drumstick heads of flowers vary from pure white to deep rose-red. There are several named forms, but self-sown seedlings provide sufficient variation if you begin with a good colour form. The foliage is tough and strong – almost coarse – with the flowerheads rising from the centre of a tuft in early spring.

They thrive best in moist loam, but would do well planted at the base of a rock in the cool. This is a striking plant, and a must for beginners.

Propagation is best done by seed in midsummer. Sow in normal soil, and the young plants will be ready by the next spring. Any good colour forms should be increased by root cuttings taken in September.

Take care
Plant where it can naturalize. 106♦

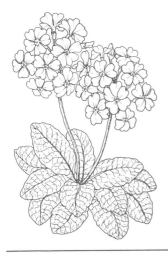

Primula frondosa

- Semi-shade
- Peaty, leafy soil
- Herbaceous

A neat, pretty little plant that forms a rosette of attractive grey-green leaves with farina (mealy coating) on the undersides. Flower stems up to 15cm (6in) bear masses of pink-lilac to red-purple 1cm (0.4in) wide miniature primrose flowers, sometimes with a white eye.

P. frondosa is found near melting snow by shady cliffs in the Balkans, and so in cultivation prefers a moist soil, lightly shaded. It thrives in a west- or east-facing peat bed or in the lee of a rock away from the direct rays of the sun.

Propagation is by seed sown in late summer or late winter. Fresh seed is best, as in all the primrose family; pot up in the spring, and plant in early autumn.

Take care
Although it likes a moist site, this plant does not like it too damp.

Primula juliae

- Cool situation
- Leafy soil
- Evergreen

The type species forms mats of heart-shaped leaves on a tangle of underground stems or rhizomes. These in turn produce clusters of short-stemmed magenta flowers, about 10cm (4in) tall, which nestle in the tufts of leaves.

It is a very easy plant on most soils, given a cool site, but its preference is for a leafy humus. It has hybridized with other species to form some well-known hybrids: *Primula* × 'Garryarde' with bronze flushed leaves, or the well-known 'Wanda', with claret-coloured flowers sometimes appearing in midwinter.

Propagation is by division in late summer, planting direct into the garden or potting up for distribution. The roots may well be entangled and will need firm pulling apart, particularly in older specimens.

Take care
Keep damper than *P. frondosa*. 106♦

Primula sieboldii 'Alba'

- ● Cool situation
- ● Non-limey soil
- ● Herbaceous

Primula viallii

- ● Light shade
- ● Light rich soil
- ● Herbaceous

The Asiatic primulas are sometimes a challenge to cultivation, but although *P. sieboldii* appears to be a tender plant by virtue of its soft-looking leaves, it is quite hardy, dying right down each winter and producing its soft crinkly leaves with scalloped edges in early summer. The flower stalks, varying from 10 to 30cm (4-12in), bear umbels of rose-pink flowers, 2-4cm (0.8-1.6in) across, in midsummer. There are several colour forms, through to white ('Alba'), which is illustrated; some have crinkled petals. All prefer light shade and a well-drained soil rich in humus.

Propagation can be by division in early spring as growth begins, or by fresh seed sown immediately it is gathered. This will provide young plants quickly, ready to over-winter in pots or boxes and be planted out the following spring.

The comparison of this plant to an 'elegant Red Hot Poker' is apt, for the distinctive upright flower spikes have just that appearance. The scarlet buds open to reveal small lavender flowers; the 7-12cm (2.75-4.75in) long dense spikes are on a flower stalk of a total height of 30cm (12in) and appear in midsummer. The narrow lanceolate leaves form a tuft and the flowers are slightly scented.

Although this plant needs a moist soil, it also requires the ground to be well-drained – not always an easy combination to achieve, and herein lies one of the difficulties of its cultivation.

Propagation is exactly as for *P. sieboldii* – either by division or from seed.

Take care
Make sure this plant never dries out.

Take care
Must not be too dry or too wet. 107♦

Ptilotrichum spinosum
- Full sun
- Any good well-drained soil
- Evergreen shrublet

This plant comes from the rocks and screes of southern France and central and southern Spain. It has a wildly confused nomenclature, and may be listed as *Alyssum spinosum*. It forms a much-branched little shrub with small grey leaves, which can spread up to 40cm (16in). The small flowers are white or pink, and you should see it in flower before purchasing, if the preferable pink form is required.

This species is easy to cultivate; it is not fussy about its requirements, apart from needing some sunshine and good drainage.

Seed is the best method of propagation, but germination is not easy, so keep a look-out for self-sown seedlings, which can be dug up and potted in early autumn: but take care not to damage the root system too much.

Take care
This is not a plant for a cool shady damp spot. 107♦

Pulsatilla vulgaris
- Open situation
- Likes some lime
- Herbaceous

One of the glories of alpine pastures and chalk downs, from England to the Ukraine. In cultivation this plant makes bushy clumps, and when mature these produce up to two dozen dark to pale purple cup-shaped flowers on 25-30cm (10-12in) stems; the flowers can be as wide as 8.5cm (3.3in). The foliage is hairy and deeply cut, resembling a fern or carrot leaf, and after flowering there appear most attractive fluffy seedheads.

This plant is very easy to cultivate, given a sunny spot and a good soil, but it appreciates some lime, which could be given as drainage in the form of limestone chippings.

Propagation is easy by seed, which germinates quite quickly after midsummer sowing. Water well until the foliage dies down, and plant out the following spring. Good forms can be increased by root cuttings.

Take care
Do not move this plant, once it is established.

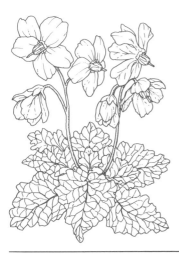

Ramonda myconi

- Semi-shade
- Acid soil
- Evergreen

Ranunculus ficaria 'Flore Plena'

(Double lesser celandine)
- Open or semi-shaded site
- Damp leafy soil
- Herbaceous

This plant is found growing on rocks in the Pyrenees, where it makes flat rosettes of slightly woolly dark green crinkled leaves. The flat-faced 2.5-4cm (1-1.6in) wide flowers appear on 10-15cm (4-6in) stems in late spring. They are lilac-blue with prominent golden stamens.

This is one of the plants that benefit from being planted on their side to prevent winter wetness from nestling in the hairy rosettes. It is an ideal plant for a north-facing aspect, planted in a rock crevice or between peat blocks. Though it likes a leafy soil, it must have good drainage.

If you want this plant in quantity, seed is the best method of propagation; you may then get some of the pink- or white-flowered forms germinating. Otherwise propagate by leaf cuttings as described under *Haberlea*.

The common British lesser celandine is far too invasive to be considered for planting in the garden, but it has some attractive colour forms – white, creamy yellow and copper. It also has a double form, 'Flore Plena', which is a rich double yellow, and less badly behaved than the type species. The flat glossy heart-shaped leaves are attractive, with silver and mahogany mottling.

This species should be planted in the dampest corner in a leafy soil; it does not mind some sun or mild shade.

Propagation is by division at almost any time of the year, provided the plants can be kept moist.

Take care
Not for a hot sunny alkaline soil. 108♦

Take care
Must not be allowed to dry out. 109♦

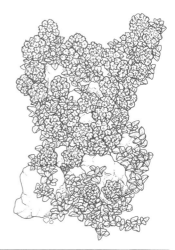

Ranunculus gramineus

- Open, sunny site
- Any soil
- Herbaceous

Raoulia australis

- Sunny position
- Well-drained soil
- Ground cover

Most buttercups require a fairly damp situation to grow happily, but this species from the mountains of southern Europe does very well in a sunny, well-drained spot with some moisture available. The foliage is narrow and glaucous blue; and the large (2cm/0.8in) flowers are a clear citron-yellow, on 20-30cm (8-12in) stems. These are freely borne over quite a long period from late spring until midsummer.

Although some purists suggest that this plant is too tall for the rock garden, it deserves a place on, say, the scree, where it will give some required height.

Propagation is either by seed sown in late winter or by division of the dormant root in early autumn. The plant is reported to benefit from division every three years.

This mat-forming plant from New Zealand is easy to cultivate as long as it is given a sunny well-drained position. It does not object to lime in the soil, but may suffer from excessive water on the leaves.

The foliage makes a prostrate silvery carpet no taller than 1cm (0.4in), and the minute pale sulphur-yellow flowers appear in early summer. The foliage is much the more important feature of this plant; it would pay to place a sheet of glass over the mat in winter.

Propagation is by division in late summer or early autumn; pot up the divisions in a gritty soil, ready for over-wintering in a frame, and plant out the following spring.

Take care
Does not need a wet situation. 109♦

Take care
Avoid excessive moisture on foliage.

Rhododendron 'Blue Tit'
- Semi-shade
- Acid soil
- Evergreen shrub

Rhodohypoxis baurii
- Sunny position
- Well-drained peaty soil
- Bulbous

To choose just one of the dozens of dwarf rhododendrons is unfair to this outstanding genus, with its wide variation of form, colour and size. There are so many colourful hybrids available.

The small-leaved deciduous azaleas such as 'Hinomayo' are suitable for a small rock garden when young, but are too large when mature. 'Blue Tit' is a hybrid of *R. impeditum* that flowers in early spring and requires an open or semi-shaded position in acid leaf-mould; as all rhododendron roots are shallow, it benefits from an annual mulch of leaf-mould.

The simplest method of propagation is by cuttings of young wood, taken with a heel just after flowering and inserted in the peat frame.

It was long thought that this dwarf bulb from the Drakensberg Mountains of South Africa was not too hardy, but it has now been in cultivation long enough to prove otherwise. Tufts of pale green hairy linear leaves appear in late spring, followed by the distinctive flat pink flowerheads with overlapping petals, which are just above the leaves and about 8cm (3.2in) tall.

This plant thrives in sunshine and a warm pocket at the base of some rocks, but it is surprising how well it will tolerate extreme winter conditions. There are some good colour forms in circulation, from pale to deep rose, and there is a particularly good clear white.

Propagation is simply by division: lift the clumps of bulbs after flowering in late summer, separate and replant the larger ones, potting up the smaller bulbs for later planting. Seed can be sown in March.

Take care
Never plant rhododendrons on an alkaline soil. 110◆

Take care
This plant does not like wet conditions. 110-111◆

Roscoea cautleoides
- **Light shade**
- **Cool soil**
- **Herbaceous**

Sagina procumbens 'Aurea'
(Pearlwort)
- **Open situation**
- **Any well-drained soil**
- **Ground cover**

It has been said that roscoeas hardly qualify as alpine plants, but by common usage on rock gardens they merit inclusion in this list. Of them all, *R. cautleoides* is probably the most handsome. Its mid-green lanceolate leaves reach from 30-40cm (12-16in) and a profusion of soft luminous yellow orchid-like flowers appear just above this foliage in summer.

They prefer a cool situation, the peat garden being an appropriate spot where they can enjoy the moist peaty soil.

Propagation is by division of the dormant roots in spring. Self-sown seedlings can be potted up in late summer, or seed sown in late winter, keeping the young plants shaded during the summer. The fleshy roots do not like being confined in a small pot, so do not delay planting out.

Anywhere else in the garden, pearlwort is a pesky weed. But *S. procumbens* 'Aurea', with its attractive golden foliage, has a place on the rock garden, where it can be allowed to invade an area about 30cm (12in) in diameter. If you want to make an alpine lawn of low-growing plants, this is a candidate. The flowers are minute, off-white and totally insignificant.

It seems to tolerate a wide variety of soils, but you should incorporate some drainage in the form of grit or very sharp sand in the top layer of soil. It is very tolerant as a cover for the smaller early-flowering crocus or narcissus bulbs.

Propagation is by division at almost any time, but is best in early autumn; plant out direct or over-winter in a pot.

Take care
Plant roscoeas deeply and they will survive hard winters. 110♦

Take care
Do not plant in shade, where it may be drawn up. 112♦

Salix arbuscula

(Dwarf willow)
- **Open situation but not too sunny in summer.**
- **Not too dry a soil**
- **Deciduous shrub**

There are a number of dwarf willows suitable for the rock garden, mostly from the European Alps. Creeping woody stems throw up a number of other stems, which end up making a gnarled bush in time, with a maximum height of 40-45cm (16-18in) and a spread of 60cm (2ft). The leaves are a deep green, and glaucous beneath; the slender grey catkins appear in mid-spring.

This shrub needs a moist soil of any composition, but not too rich, in an open situation; it does not like the direct hot sunshine of midsummer, and requires moisture all the year round.

Propagation is by cuttings with a heel, taken from midsummer to early autumn and inserted in a sandy frame. Make sure the tips are pinched out, to encourage bushy growth.

Take care
Do not plant in too hot or dry a situation. 112♦

Sanguinaria canadensis 'Flore Pleno'

(Blood-root)
- **Sun or semi-shade**
- **Leafy soil**
- **Herbaceous**

Related to the poppy, this is a genus with a single species, from North America. The common name refers to the red liquid that oozes from the root when cut. In spring, heads of double white flowers about 10cm (4in) tall poke through the soil, followed by the palmate greyish green leaves, which die down by the end of summer. The flowers of this double form last longer than the rather thin-looking single flowers of the species.

Once planted, preferably in a leafy soil, they should not be disturbed; they enjoy either a sunny situation or some shade.

Propagation of the double form can only be by division in March, when great care should be taken. The plants are not too happy in pots, and should preferably be planted out in a leafy frame.

Take care
Make sure this plant is labelled. 129♦

Saponaria ocymoides

(Soapwort)
- **Open sunny situation**
- **Well-drained soil**
- **Evergreen**

Saxifraga burserana

- **Open situation, but summer shade**
- **Very gritty soil**
- **Evergreen**

An invaluable plant for every rock garden or rock wall, where its prostrate mat looks well cascading down over the rocks. It is a plant of shingle banks in the Alps of south-western and south central Europe, which indicates its need for good drainage. The mats can be 30cm (12in) across and are covered with dozens of 1cm (0.4in) wide pink flowers that appear from mid- to late summer.

There are two selected forms: 'Compacta', which is slower-growing and less vigorous; and 'Rubra Compacta', with rich carmine flowers. They are all easy to cultivate.

Propagation is very easy by soft cuttings in summer, taken from non-flowering wood and placed in a sand frame. It is necessary to stop the young plants at least twice to get a tidy young plant.

S. burserana is valuable for its early flowers, produced in late winter or early spring. It forms a dense cushion of blue-grey lanceolate leaves, which is an attraction in itself, with the 2.5cm (1in) wide solid-textured white flowers covering the cushion on 5cm (2in) long stalks. It has several named varieties: 'Brookside' and 'Gloria' have larger flowers; 'Sulphurea' is soft yellow.

This saxifrage belongs to a section of the genus called Kabischia. All members of this section require a well-drained soil, which can be a mixture of leaf-mould, loam and limestone chippings. It is helpful to top-dress around the plants, pushing chippings under the cushions.

Propagation by division tends to destroy the compact cushions, so cuttings, which of necessity are no longer than 1-1.5cm (0.4-0.6in), are put in the sand frame in midsummer and kept shaded and well watered.

Take care
Give this plant room to expand. 129♦

Take care
Dislikes midday sun in summer.

Saxifraga cochlearis 'Minor'

- Open position
- Well-drained limestone scree
- Evergreen

The encrusted saxifrages form rosettes of grey-green leaves that are often attractively encrusted with spots of lime around the edges. *S. cochlearis* is found on limestone rocks in the Maritime Alps, which gives a lead to its requirements in cultivation: a well-drained situation, ideally on scree.

The form 'Minor' is ideal for planting in a trough, and forms an extremely neat hummock of grey-leaved rosettes, from which shoot sprays of 1.5cm (0.6in) wide milk-white flowers in early summer, no taller than 10cm (4in). This is a most attractive plant.

Propagation is by detaching the side rosettes in August, preferably with some roots attached, and potting them on into a limey soil; or they can be planted out direct.

Saxifraga × 'Peter Pan'

- Semi-shaded situation
- Neutral soil
- Evergreen

Saxifraga moschata, of which 'Peter Pan' is a hybrid, occurs across Europe from the Pyrenees to the Caucasus, but is rarely grown in cultivation, being represented more by its various forms and hybrids. 'Peter Pan' is one such, producing neat low hummocks of bright green mossy leaves, from which are produced crimson flowers about 1cm (0.4in) across, on stalks shorter than the type at 8-10cm (3.2-4in). It may spread to 30cm (12in). It prefers to be out of the direct rays of the sun, so some protection is helpful – the dappled shade from a deciduous tree, for instance. 'Cloth of Gold' is another variety, and has clear yellow foliage that burns badly in the sun, so fuller shade is necessary.

Propagation is by removing small offsets in late summer and potting them up in a neutral soil.

Take care
This plant needs good drainage and a limey soil. 130♦

Take care
Make certain this plant avoids the intense sun of midsummer.

Above: **Sanguinaria canadensis 'Flore Pleno'**
A striking plant, with pure white double flowers that appear very early in spring. Do not disturb. 126♦

Below: **Saponaria ocymoides**
The soapwort is happy to cascade over a stone wall or rocks, where the mass of pink flowers can be seen to best advantage. 127♦

Left: **Saxifraga cochlearis 'Minor'**
The illustration shows only the flower of this encrusted saxifrage; its silver-edged rosettes form a tight clump. It is happy growing in tufa and is most appropriate for a trough. 128♦

Right: **Saxifraga umbrosa 'Elliott's Variety'**
This is a dwarf version of the rather gross 'London Pride'. Both will grow almost anywhere with ease. 145♦

Below: **Saxifraga cotyledon 'Southside Seedling'**
There are several named varieties of this saxifrage from the European Alps, all of which make excellent crevice plants. The touch of pink adds distinction here. 145♦

Above: **Scilla tubergeniana**
It is doubtful if the new name of this bulb, S. mischtschenkoana, will ever be recognized by gardeners, so the old name of this early bulb is retained. An adaptable plant. 146♦

Right: **Sedum spathulifolium 'Cappa Blanca'**
A most distinctive stonecrop, grown mainly for its intense grey foliage, which gives interest for most of the year. Grow in sunshine. 147♦

Below: **Sedum acre 'Aureum'**
A contrasting foliage colour is provided by this biting stonecrop or wallpepper. It does tend to spread but is controllable. The flowers are of no importance. 146♦

Left: **Silene schafta**
*This useful late-flowering plant from
the Caucasus has flowers that are
produced in profusion when the rock
garden is waiting for the autumn
colour to arrive. It loves full sunshine
and is very easy to grow.* 148♦

Right:
Sisyrinchium bermudianum
*Its common name, 'blue-eyed
grass', is aptly descriptive. It is late
flowering and has a tendency to seed
about, but this is no great
disadvantage.* 148♦

Below: **Solidago brachystachys**
*An early autumn-flowering plant that
is a miniature version of golden rod.
It rarely exceeds 15cm (6in) and
does well in any soil, producing its
golden flowerheads.* 149♦

Left: **Syringa meyeri 'Palibin'**
*This may also be found listed as
S.palibiniana. It is a miniature lilac,
reaching in due course a height of
1.5m (5ft), but over a very long
period, so it can be used safely in
small gardens.* 150♦

Right: **Teucrium pyrenaicum**
*The Pyrenean germander thrives in a
sunny position and is a plant that
tolerates alkaline conditions, forming
a neat mat of crinkly leaves and
creamy flowers.* 151♦

Below: **Thymus × 'Doone Valley'**
*The illustration shows a mass of
typical pink thyme flowers, but this
particular hybrid of unknown
parentage has quite outstanding
variegated foliage.* 151♦

Above: **Thymus serpyllum**
The thymes are well known for their
scented foliage and so are good for
planting on terraces where they will
be trodden upon to bring out the
pleasant aroma. 152◆

Above: **Trillium sessile**
A North American woodlander that is happy in the cool conditions of a peat bed. It will thrive in other soil types, provided it does not dry out in the summer months. 152♦

Below: **Tropaeolum polyphyllum**
This quite spectacular species from Chile produces long stems clothed in grey leaves, and with yellow nasturtium-like flowers appearing en masse in midsummer. 153♦

Above: **Tulipa greigii**
This parent of many hybrids is still worthwhile in itself on the rock garden in spring. 153♦

Left: **Tulipa sylvestris**
An easily grown species, but sometimes not very free-flowering. It is suitable for naturalizing. 155♦

Right: **Tulipa marjolettii**
Perhaps a mite too tall for some rock gardens, this is a sturdy species that does not flop. 154♦

Above: **Tulipa tarda**
This does well in an open position, where the flowers will respond to the sun in early spring even on comparatively cold days. It can have up to five flowers on a stem. 155♦

Left: **Uvularia perfoliata**
This relation of the lily spreads by underground rhizomes. It prefers a cool corner and is happy on the peat bed, where it should be marked well because the foliage dies down early in the season. 156♦

Right: **Veronica prostrata**
A useful ground cover plant in a mild way, that produces a mass of small blue flowers in early summer. There are several named cultivars that have arisen over the years. 157♦

Above: **Veronica teucrium 'Trehane'**
A distinctive veronica, with an unusual combination of yellow foliage and blue flowers. 157♦

Below: **Verbascum × 'Letitia'**
This hybrid between V. dumulosum *and* V. spinosum *is a showy plant in flower, and justifiably popular for its good behaviour.* 158♦

Saxifraga 'Southside Seedling'

- Open situation
- Neutral soil
- Evergreen

Another of the encrusted saxifrages but with larger leaves and rosettes, from the mountains of Europe from the Pyrenees through to Lapland and Iceland. It grows in the crevices of granite rocks, and so requires good drainage in cultivation, but not in the form of limestone chippings as for other saxifrages.

There are many geographical variants and garden hybrids, of which 'Southside Seedling' is one: it has strap-shaped leaves forming the rosettes, from which in summer are produced the arching sprays of white flowers, heavily spotted with red, on 30cm (12in) stems.

Propagate by dividing up the clump after flowering in late summer: plant the rosettes out direct or pot them up. Seed will not come true, but they can be tried.

Take care
This plant is not as desperate for lime as others in the encrusted section of the genus. 130-131♦

Saxifraga umbrosa 'Elliott's Variety'

- Shady situation
- Any soil
- Evergreen

'Elliott's Variety' is a miniature version of the well-known 'London Pride', which thrives in any shady corner, damp or dry. It has neat foliage and deep rose flowers on 10-15cm (4-6in) stems in early summer.

This plant is not invasive, spreading not much beyond 20-30cm (8-12in). It is extremely useful for seemingly impossible corners in the rock garden.

Propagation is by division in early autumn, planting out direct or potting up individual rooted rosettes if you want quantity.

Take care
This plant does not enjoy full sun. 131♦

Scilla tubergeniana
- **Any situation**
- **Any soil**
- **Bulbous**

This is one of those accommodating plants that will grow anywhere on the rock garden, and is also useful under shrubs elsewhere in the garden. It is one of the first to push through in late winter and is thus especially valuable. It flowers over a long period and is a native of the southern Caucasus. Strictly speaking, its name is now *S. mischtschenkoana*, but it is only rarely that you will find it listed under this entirely unpronounceable name. The pale blue flowers, streaked with darker blue, emerge as buds before the leaves, and immediately open; they eventually reach a height of 15cm (6in).

Seed is rarely produced, but the bulbs increase well, and can be lifted and divided.

Sedum acre 'Aureum'
- **Sunny situation**
- **Any soil**
- **Evergreen**

The native yellow stonecrop is a rather invasive plant, best left to inhabit the crevices of old walls, where the yellow flowers make a bright splash of colour. The form 'Aureum' is still relatively active, but has the added attraction of golden yellow tips to its leafy shoots in spring and yellowy green the rest of the year.

This is an excellent subject for the alpine lawn and can be under-planted with bulbs. The flowers are yellow as in the species, but not of such importance in view of the useful foliage. It is not fussy about either soil or situation, though perhaps providing more foliage colour in a sunny spot.

Propagation is no problem: almost any piece of the plant that is broken off will root, and division is possible at most times of year.

Take care
The foliage dies down early, so label its position. 132♦

Take care
Do not plant coloured foliage in deep shape. 132♦

Sedum spathulifolium 'Cappa Blanca'

- Sunny position
- Any soil
- Evergreen

S. spathulifolium is a widely grown plant native to north-west America, where it inhabits rocky ledges in the drier foothills from British Columbia down to California. It makes dense mats of grey-green leaves in fleshy rosettes and is a good carpeting plant, spreading to 30cm (12in) or more and producing flat yellow flowerheads, 5-8cm (2-3.2in) across in midsummer on 10cm (4in) stems.

The form 'Cappa Blanca' is from Cape Blanco in Southern Oregon and has silvery grey foliage that is slightly smaller than the species. It behaves exactly like the species, and is a most attractive plant. Two other forms – 'Purpureum', with larger purple leaves, and 'Aureum', with leaves tinted yellow, but less vigorous – are in circulation.

Propagation, as with most sedums, is easy: by division at any time or, if quantity is required, by detaching single rosettes and potting them up.

Take care
Although it is not violently invasive, allow room to expand. 133♦

Sempervivum arachnoideum

- Full sunshine
- Any well-drained soil
- Evergreen

The houseleeks are useful hardy plants for covering an area of the rock garden, but some can be rather gross for the smaller garden, whereas the cobweb houseleek, *S. arachnoideum,* in its varying forms can look more appropriate. The rosettes are 2-4cm (0.8-1.6in) wide and criss-crossed with white hairs that have the look of a cobweb. The total height of the plant is no more than 1-1.5cm (0.4-0.6in) and it can spread up to 30cm (12in). The 2cm (0.8in) wide bright rose-red flowers appear on 15cm (6in) stems in midsummer. When grown slightly starved the rosettes become very tight and hard.

Propagation is simple by detaching a rosette and inserting it in sand, if it does not already possess a rooting system.

Take care
Never over-feed or plant in a shady corner where it can become drawn.

Silene schafta
- **Any sunny position**
- **Any soil**
- **Evergreen**

This most accommodating plant has few dislikes and will give of its best in most situations. Mid-green lanceolate leaves form a tuft that spreads up to 30cm (12in) and produces sprays of rose-magenta flowers on 10-15cm (4-6in) stems over a very long period from midsummer to early autumn. Although it is easily grown, there is a slight coarseness about the plant that does not rank it among the aristocrats of the rock garden.

Propagation is fairly quick by seed sown in late winter; pot the seedlings up in early spring ready for planting out in early summer. Alternatively, cuttings taken in midsummer and placed in a sand frame make specimens ready for planting in autumn.

Sisyrinchium bermudianum
(Blue-eyed grass)
- **Full sun**
- **Any good garden soil**
- **Evergreen**

Plants that seed about can sometimes be unpopular. However, although *S. bermudianum* is guilty of this habit, it is one that can be lived with. The 15cm (6in) upright flat iris-like foliage is useful for giving some height to a flat area on the rock garden. Some of the leaves are in fact disguised flower stalks and small satiny blue flowers appear at the leaf tips from early summer.

This species is very easy to cultivate, growing even in shaded situations on the peat bed if you do not watch it. It is also very useful in a paved area where it can seed in the cracks.

Its habit of seeding about makes propagation easy: just gather up the seedlings and pot them on. Alternatively, you can sow seed in midwinter, or divide in early spring or early autumn.

Take care
There are no problems at all with this easy plant! 134♦

Take care
Do not plant where the self-sown seedlings will be a nuisance. 135♦

Soldanella alpina

- Cool situation
- Moist leafy soil
- Evergreen

This is one of the delights of the Alps when it is seen pushing through the melting snow. A spreading mat, up to 25cm (10in) wide, is formed by the rounded kidney-shaped leaves. The flowers appear in spring and are mauve-coloured deeply fringed hanging bells, one to three on a 7.5cm (3in) stem.

They appreciate a moist, cool situation, in the peat garden or perhaps a gritty, leafy soil; in nature they prefer limestone areas. They have a reputation for being shy-flowered, possibly because the buds are formed very early in winter beneath the leaves, and are a favourite dish for slugs, which may not be seen devouring them. Winter wetness is also a deterrent, so some protection could be given.

Propagation is by careful division in midsummer, making sure that each division has some fibrous root. Pot into a gritty leafy soil containing some limestone chippings.

Take care
Protect this plant from slugs.

Solidago brachystachys

(Dwarf golden rod)
- Sunny situation
- Any well-drained soil
- Herbaceous

This is a dubious name: some authorities believe it is a form of *S. virgaurea,* the wild golden rod. What is undeniable is its dwarf habit and suitability for the rock garden, and that it is a dependable plant for flowering in early autumn. It makes a small clump, which when in flower is 15-20cm (6-8in) tall; the flowers are a miniature golden-yellow version of the larger golden rod. It does well in any soil, provided it has some good drainage and is in full sun.

Propagation is best by division in spring, planting direct or potting up. Seed sown in January tends to be unreliable. Beware self-sown seedlings, as they do not come true.

Take care
Although ordinary golden rod is invasive, this plant is not; but do not plant it too close to other spreading plants. 135♦

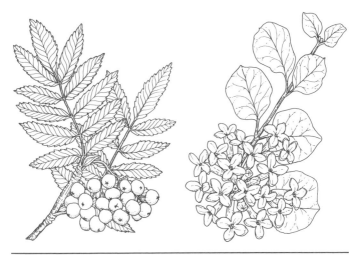

Sorbus reducta
(Pygmy mountain ash)
- **Open situation**
- **Any soil**
- **Deciduous dwarf shrub**

It is curious to have a miniature mountain ash that is suitable for the rock garden, where it will gently sucker and is well behaved enough to be planted in a trough, but in *Sorbus reducta* we have just that. It comes from Western China and Burma and is quite hardy, making a sturdy slow-growing bush 15-30cm (6-12in) tall, with typical mountain ash foliage and terminal clusters of white flowers 1cm (0.4in) wide appearing in midsummer. The 5-7mm (0.2-0.3in) wide rose-pink berries are freely produced in autumn, at which time the leaves turn red-purple, so it is a worthwhile plant for several reasons. It prefers a well-drained soil, but is otherwise not fussy.

Propagation is either by fresh seed sown in autumn, or by careful division in spring.

Take care
Do not plant anything nearby that will interfere with the gentle journeying of this shrub.

Syringa meyeri 'Palibin'
((Dwarf lilac)
- **Open situation**
- **Any soil**
- **Deciduous shrub**

Although reported eventually to reach a spread and height of 1.5m (5ft), I have yet to see one that has reached those dimensions. In 11 years our plant is 1.2m (4ft) high by 1m (39in) across. It makes a twiggy bush, which blooms freely at the usual time for lilacs, in early summer, producing slightly scented lavender-purple flower panicles.

It is not fussy about soil, though it prefers not to grow in wet boggy conditions. It requires no pruning.

Propagation is by heel cuttings, 7-10cm (2.75-4in) long, taken from non-flowering shoots in midsummer. Insert these in a peat and sand frame. If mist propagation is available, this is a help. Pot the rooted cuttings in John Innes No. 2 compost.

Take care
Although it takes some time to reach its ultimate height, allow space when planting. 136◀

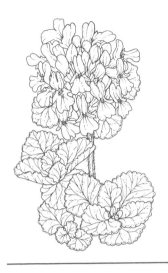
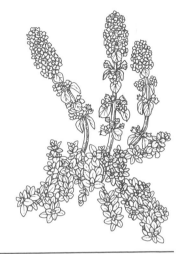

Teucrium pyrenaicum

- Sunny exposure
- Light, well-drained soil
- Evergreen

Thymus × 'Doone Valley'

- Open, sunny situation
- Any soil
- Evergreen

Some shrubby members of this genus have aromatic foliage, but not so *T. pyrenaicum*, which is a trailing plant with crinkly woolly leaves forming a neat mat about 30cm (12in) across. It is low-growing, and when in flower is only 5-8cm (2-3.2in) high. The flowers are curiously hooded, mauve and cream, in flat heads about 2.5cm (1in) across, and they appear from mid- to late summer.

This plant needs a well-drained soil, preferably on the light side, and a sunny situation. It is basically hardy, but may succumb to a particularly wet cold winter.

Propagation is by division in spring; pot up rooted rosettes into John Innes No. 2 compost and these will be ready for planting in six to eight weeks.

All the thymes love the sun in an open position and are not fussy over soils, although obviously they would not be happy in waterlogged conditions. They form flat mats, are ideal for the alpine house and can be under-planted with bulbs. The foliage is aromatic and does well where it can be stepped on to draw out its fragrance.

'Doone Valley' is of doubtful parentage but of undoubted worth, with its olive-green leaves flecked with golden spots. Rounded heads of lavender flowers are borne on 10cm (4in) stems in summer.

Propagation is by division in late summer; pot up the small pieces or plant them out direct.

Take care
A pane of glass over this plant in a wet winter may assist it. 137♦

Take care
Do not plant 'Doone Valley' in shade, or it will lose its variegation. 136-137♦

Thymus serpyllum

(Thyme)
- ● Open sunny situation
- ● Any soil
- ● Evergreen

This forms a prostrate mat, perfect for the alpine lawn and for under-planting with bulbs. It is a very variable plant, both in its native habitats throughout Europe and in cultivation, where there are several named forms. The mats can spread to 60cm (2ft) or more, but are beautiful when smothered with the 1cm (0.4in) heads of flowers that range from pink to rich rose.

Of the named forms 'Coccineum', with deep red flowers, is outstanding; 'Minus' is useful for sinks and troughs because of its compact habit; and 'Silver Queen' has silver and green variegated foliage. If white flowers are to your liking, there is 'Albus', which also has paler foliage.

Propagation is by division in spring or autumn, potting up the divisions or planting direct.

Trillium sessile

- ● Cool position
- ● Moisture-holding soil
- ● Herbaceous

It is hard to believe that trilliums belong to the lily family, because they are so different in looks. Strong stems emerge, 15-30cm (6-12in) tall, on top of which are three dark green oval leaves, marbled grey. Where these three leaves meet, the stemless purple-pointed flowers appear in spring.

They are long-lived plants if given the right conditions: a cool, shady position that never dries out, with a leafy, peaty soil, although they will accept a heavier soil with equanimity.

Propagation is by division in late summer; make certain that the roots do not dry out when they are dug up. Plant out directly, or pot up in a leafy soil. Seed can be sown in spring in a fine leafy compost.

Take care
Remember its spreading habit and allow plenty of room. 138♦

Take care
Never plant in full sun or allow to dry out. It needs a cool, shady spot. 139♦

Tropaeolum polyphyllum
- **Sunny situation**
- **Deep, well-drained soil**
- **Herbaceous**

This is a spectacular species that seems difficult to establish, but it is worth the effort, as it is so distinctive and showy. It is a tuberous-rooted perennial, which sends up long trailing or arching stems of grey leaves, in the axils of which are produced large rich yellow nasturtium-like flowers in early and mid-summer. It dies away after flowering and is likely to come up in a completely different spot the following year.

The secret of success is to plant the tuber at least 30cm (12in) deep, in a position where its trailing stems can hang down over a rock or wall. Its hardiness has long been proven.

Once the plant is established, propagation is simple, by digging up the tubers as required.

Take care
Plant deep, and allow space for this desirable plant to spread. 139♦

Tulipa greigii
- **Sunny position**
- **Well-drained soil**
- **Bulbous**

The species tulips have a charm of their own, which makes the larger garden hybrids look out of place on the rock garden. *Tulipa greigii*, which has been the parent of many showy hybrids, has brilliant orange-scarlet cup-shaped flowers, up to 15cm (6in) in diameter, on 20-25cm (8-10in) stems, and grey-green leaves with purple-brown veining. Most of the hybrids have this distinctive veining.

They like a sunny well-drained situation and may settle down for some years, but are rarely long-lived unless lifted and stored each year after flowering. Planting takes place each autumn. They can be cultivated in pots but still need to be re-potted during the dormant season in summer.

Propagation of the true species can be from seed sown in late winter; otherwise, increase in the bulb must be relied on.

Take care
Do not plant in shade, and lift after flowering. 140♦

153

Tulipa kaufmanniana
(Water lily tulip)
- Sunny position
- Well-drained soil
- Bulbous

This tulip's compact habit suits a rock garden. A rosette of grey basal leaves is formed in early spring, from which appear the yellow-tinged creamy flowers, flushed pink on the outside. The following varieties are recommended: the aptly named 'The First' (15cm/6in) with carmine-red flowers edged with white, opening to ivory-white; 'Stresa' (18cm/7in), yellow inside, with a blood-red blotch at the base, the outside flushed red and margined yellow; 'Shakespeare' (12cm/4.75in), a free-flowering variety with a mixture of salmon, apricot and orange. These cover a flowering period from late winter to spring and are extremely colourful.

Propagation is by increase of the bulbs for the hybrids, and by seed for *T. kaufmanniana* itself, sown in late winter.

Take care
Lift and store after flowering.

Tulipa marjolettii
- Sunny situation
- Well-drained soil
- Bulbous

Although rather tall (35-45cm/14-18in) for the smaller rock garden, this tulip has much grace. It is reputed not to be a true species, but a garden hybrid from southern France. It has grey leaves and soft primrose-yellow flowers slightly stained red on the exterior of the petals. These appear in late spring.

The bulb frame is an excellent place for tulips. This structure, usually raised up off the ground, is covered by tall frame lights to allow for growth. The lights are removed during the growing period in spring, and replaced when the foliage has died down, to simulate the summer baking the bulbs would receive in the wild. The frames are removed in early autumn for some moisture, and then replaced for the winter; open them on fine frost-free days. An annual feeding of bone-meal in autumn before watering is a help.

Take care
Do not water the bulb frame during the summer months.141▶

Tulipa sylvestris
- **Open situation**
- **Any soil**
- **Bulbous**

This is not quite such a free-flowering species, but is suitable for both the rock garden and borders, and will naturalize in woodland conditions or grass. It has narrow grey-green leaves and scented yellow flowers on 30cm (12in) stems. When fully open the flowers are 6-8cm (2.4-3.2in) across. There is a form from northern Iran that flowers more freely, offered as *T.s.* var. *tabriz*.

Propagation is by increased bulbs or by seed sown in late winter. If germination does not take place the first year, then the seed pots should be left outside another winter for a frosting.

Tulipa tarda
- **Sunny position**
- **Any well-drained soil**
- **Bulbous**

This tulip can be left *in situ* during the dormant season. It thrives in a sunny situation: on a fine day in late spring, its flowers open wide, looking flat and starry in the midday sun. The flowering stem is only 10-12cm (4-4.75in) tall, rising from a virtually flat rosette of narrow green leaves. There are up to five blooms on a stem, and it is one of the most widely and easily grown of all the tulip species.

Propagation is by seed sown in late winter, or by an increase in bulbs, which can be lifted after flowering for this purpose.

Take care
Does not demand a sunny situation or need to be lifted annually. 140♦

Take care
This bulb does not have to be lifted and stored each year. 142-143♦

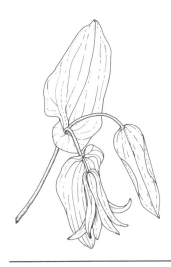

Uvularia perfoliata
(Throat-wort)
- **Light shade**
- **Leafy soil**
- **Herbaceous**

This small genus of hardy plants, from the woods of North America, is related to the lily, and has a rhizomatous root system. They are ideal for a shady part of the rock or peat garden. A single upright stem, about 20-25cm (8-10in) tall, appears in late spring, with sessile pointed heart-shaped leaves on the upper part. Numerous pendent pale yellow narrow bell-shaped flowers are found, singly or in pairs, at the tips of branchlets. The leaves are perfoliate, ie the main stem appears to pass through them.

The best time for propagation is in summer when the plants can be divided and potted up in leafy soil and kept moist and shaded. Division in mid-autumn is possible but brings the possibility of greater loss in winter.

Vancouveria hexandra
(Inside-out flower)
- **Light shade**
- **Cool leafy soil**
- **Herbaceous**

This is a plant for the shady corner of the rock or peat garden where it can romp through the leafy soil; it is a good ground cover plant. The slender-stalked, heart-shaped leaves are carried on wiry stems and are usually three-lobed. Panicles of white flowers on 23cm (9in) stems are produced in late spring. This species comes from the moist shady woods of North America and it is an excellent ground cover for small bulbs such as the wood anemone, in early spring.

Propagation is by division in spring; plant direct or into leafy soil in pots, which need to be plunged in a shaded frame.

Take care
This is not a plant for the sunny rock garden; it prefers some shade. 142♦

Take care
Mark where this plant is, and do not put it in full sunshine.

Veronica prostrata
(V. rupestris)
(Speedwell)
- ● **Open situation**
- ● **Any soil**
- ● **Evergreen**

This easy plant is invaluable on the rock garden. It is a wide-spread mat-forming plant, found from Europe across to northern Asia, but somewhat variable. The mats of mid-green leaves can spread up to 45cm (18in) with short 5-8cm (2-3.2in) spikes of deep blue flowers from early to mid-summer. It is not fussy about soil and will give a good display in either acid or alkaline conditions. It has several named varieties: 'Spode Blue' is a clear pale blue; 'Rosea' is pink; and 'Alba' is white.

Propagation is by soft cuttings taken from midsummer to early autumn; insert them in a sand frame and pot up to over-winter. It is so easy to increase that 10cm (4in) long cuttings with some old wood can be inserted in the open ground.

Take care
This plant will not benefit from too rich a soil. 143♦

Veronica teucrium 'Trehane'
- ● **Open situation**
- ● **Well-drained soil**
- ● **Herbaceous**

The true species is a good plant from southern Europe and northern Asia, but it is extremely variable. It is the smaller forms that interest the rock gardener. The plant produces a clump of dark green foliage and shortish (23-38cm/9-15in) spikes of sky-blue appear in profusion over a long period in summer.

In the form 'Trehane' the foliage is golden-yellow and this contrasts pleasantly with the blue flowers. It is not as vigorous as the species and so does not spread to much more than 20-25cm (8-10in).

Propagation is by any type of cutting from mid- to late summer; pot up when rooted, to over-winter in a cold frame.

Take care
If this plant is put in a shady place it will rapidly lose the yellow colouring of its leaves. 144♦

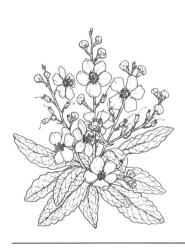

Verbascum × 'Letitia'
- **Open sunny situation**
- **Any well-drained soil**
- **Sub-shrub**

This is a hybrid between *V. dumulosum* and *V. spinosum,* discovered at the RHS Garden at Wisley, southern England, in the early 1960s, so it has not long been in cultivation, but it is already very popular. It forms a shrubby bush, with velvety grey-green leaves; the tips of the many stems produce so many racemes of clear yellow flowers, 2.5cm (1in) wide, from mid-summer onwards, that the plant is smothered in bloom. Its height and spread can reach 40cm (16in).

It does best in a sandy, well-drained soil in full sun and is excellent for the alpine house.

The best method of propagation for this plant was discovered accidentally: its roots had grown into the chippings on a greenhouse bench, and when the pot was removed the roots were broken, and those remaining sprouted leaves. So increase this plant by root cuttings.

Take care
Give this plant a good site in full sun, partially sheltered by rocks if necessary, but with plenty of air. 144►

Waldsteinia fragarioides
- **Sun or light shade**
- **Any soil**
- **Evergreen**

Although not particularly spectacular, this plant from the eastern United States has a long flowering period in the summer. It is a mildly spreading plant that is at home in any soil. It is similar to a strawberry in looks and behaviour, hence its specific name. The creeping stems produce dark green three-lobed toothed leaves, and 1cm (0.4in) wide golden-yellow flowers in early summer. It mingles quite unobtrusively with other plants, causing them no harm. If it becomes too invasive it can be controlled quite easily.

This species can be divided in late summer, by taking rooted stems at the edge of the mat and potting them in normal soil. Seed can be sown in spring. Young plants should be shaded.

Take care
This plant needs room to spread, but stronger plants could swamp it.

Index of Common Names

Picture Credits

Line artwork
The drawings in this book have been prepared by Maureen Holt, who extends her thanks to Brighton Parks and Gardens for their help with supplying reference material.
© Salamander Books Ltd.

Photographs
The photographs on pages 6 and 9 have been supplied by the author Michael Upward. All the remaining photographs have been taken by Eric Crichton exclusively for this guide.
© Salamander Books Ltd.

The publishers wish to thank the RHS Gardens, Wisley for their help with location photography.

Editorial assistance
Copy-editing and proof-reading: Maureen Cartwright.

Author's acknowledgments
The author would like to thank his friends Charles Hollidge, Joy and Jack Hulme, Chris and Freda Norton, and Frank and Mary Randall for allowing him the full freedom of their gardens for taking photographs.

Lewisia cotyledon

PRINTED IN BELGIUM BY
proost
INTERNATIONAL BOOK PRODUCTION